STAFFORD
AT WAR

1939-1945

STAFFORD
AT WAR

1939-1945

Nick Thomas

Pen & Sword
MILITARY

First published in Great Britain in 2009 by
PEN & SWORD MILITARY
an imprint of
Pen & Sword Books Limited
47 Church Street
Barnsley
S. Yorkshire
S70 2AS

ISBN 978 1 84415 943 7

A CIP catalogue record for this book
is available from the British Library

Typeset in Sabon by S L Menzies-Earl

Printed and bound in England
by CPI

Pen & Sword Books Ltd incorporates the imprints of
Pen & Sword Aviation, Pen & Sword Maritime,
Pen & Sword Military, Wharncliffe Local History, Pen & Sword Select,
Pen & Sword Military Classics and Leo Cooper.

For a complete list of Pen & Sword titles please contact:
PEN & SWORD BOOKS LIMITED
47 Church Street, Barnsley, South Yorkshire, S70 2AS, England.
E-mail: enquiries@pen-and-sword.co.uk
Website: www.pen-and-sword.co.uk

CONTENTS

Acknowledgements

This work could not have been undertaken without the active support and encouragement of many veterans. Sadly, many of the brave men and women whose accounts grace these pages have since passed away, but their legacy lives on.

I should like to acknowledge here my especial gratitude to the following, who kindly allowed me to interview them and include their stories in these pages: Mr J. Bambury, Mr Bernard Blakeman, Squadron Leader David Blomeley DFC, AFC, Mr D. Challinor, Major Clarke, Mr George Crewe, Mrs Nellie Downing, Squadron Leader Eric Johnson BEM, DFC, AFC, Chief Inspector Gordon Ferneyhough, Commander Leslie Gardiner OBE, Squadron Leader Ernest 'Gil' Gilbert, Mr E. Gosling, Mr Clifford Green, Mrs W.B. Knight, Mrs Haughton, Flight Lieutenant R. Ingar, Lady Morgan, Mr T. Myatt DFM, Wing Commander George Nelson-Edwards DFC, Mr F. Rock, Mr Michael Shelley, Mr Bill Silvester, Mr Leslie Talbot, Pilot Officer Joe Willshaw DFC, Mrs Woodward, Wing Commander Robert Wyness DFC, DFM and Captain Zdzislaw Luszowicz. I should also like to thank Mrs C. Madders for the very kind loan of the ARP log used to analyse the frequency of air raid alerts.

This book contains many chapters illustrating the gallantry and devotion to duty of local men and women serving both at home and abroad, but to me the most important people are those listed in the final chapter of this volume: Stafford's war casualties. While there is no single monument in their honour, many of them are remembered in the pages of a vellum book held in St Mary's Collegiate Church, Stafford: the churchyard has been laid out as a formal garden in their memory.

Foreword

There has long been a need for a permanent record of the county town's role during the Second World War, and this volume is as comprehensive as anyone could have wished for, drawing together accounts of the Home Front and of all of the theatres of the war. Within these pages you will find the first ever listing of the gallantry awards made to Staffordians during the war and, more poignantly, of Stafford's war dead.

When Nick began staging exhibitions and researching the stories of local people it was largely for the benefit of the veterans themselves, but gradually the reawakening of interest in the Second World War has grown. Over the years his Battle of Britain exhibition and other displays must have been seen by thousands of people of all ages, but particularly by children keen to learn about the heroism and sacrifices of a lost age.

Based on years of painstaking research and interviews, this book is a must for all seeking to learn about Stafford's part in a war in which, for a year, Great Britain and its Empire stood alone against Hitler and the Axis Powers.

At first Staffordians raised money to provide comforts for the troops. Then came the Ramsgate evacuees and service personnel who were found homes and billets in the town and quickly became a part of the Stafford 'family'. In 1942 the Americans came and their influence was soon felt, with dinner dances giving way to Hawaiian Nights and Jazz Evenings.

Everyone worked towards the same goal. Children collected hedgerow fruits, scrap metal, paper and old rags, while factory workers put in long shifts before undertaking evening duties for the war effort.

The Stafford lads who fought together did so knowing that the whole town was behind them. Those who were taken prisoner received relief parcels from the town's Comforts Fund. When the servicemen and women came back home after the war it was to a country still in the midst of rationing; the years of austerity were to be with us for nearly another decade.

Victory in Europe and Victory in Japan Days came and went, and most people just wanted to forget the war and get back to everyday life. Many veterans felt forgotten, and in truth they were by the nation, but never by their comrades-in-arms.

Through the reminiscences of local veterans, the story of *Stafford at War* can be discovered by generations to come. Many sacrificed a good education or their career and spent six years in the dedicated service of others. Most had their lives changed forever, while others paid the ultimate price for our freedom. 'We will remember them.'

Bill Silvester
President of the Stafford Branch
of the Royal British Legion

Introduction

The market town of Stafford, with a pre-war population of 31,000, sits in the heart of the West Midlands between the Potteries to the north and the Black Country to the south. As an administrative unit, the borough includes a number of outlying villages, but for the purposes of this account only the town and its suburbs are considered in detail, along with some of the local RAF airfields whose aircraft filled the skies over the county town. In addition, there were numerous civilian and military establishments close to the town, many of which also fall outside the scope of this volume. These include the Trentham Convalescent Camp, the Burntwood Emergency Hospital, the Munitions Store at Swynnerton, HMS *Fledgeling*, Swynnerton (the WRENs' Technical Training Establishment) and the USAAF Depot at Stone, to name but a few.

There were a number of PoW camps close to the county town, with some of the prisoners being sent to work on local farms and even at military establishments such as RAF Stafford. These camps included those at Hopton, Teddesley and Gnosall. In addition, there was a PoW hospital at nearby Shugborough. The Teddesley PoW camp was the scene of a mass break-out on 18 December 1944, when thirteen prisoners escaped. They were recaptured as far afield as Liverpool, Derby, Wolverhampton and Walsall, but the last fugitive to be apprehended was arrested in nearby Penkridge on Boxing Day.

The Second World War touched Stafford in many ways, with Staffordians serving in every theatre of the war, from the Home Front to the Russian convoys, and from Europe to the war against the Japanese in the Far East. Stafford's hospital cared for less seriously wounded individuals and those who required long-term care; the unfailing dedication and countless kindnesses of the doctors and nurses could fill a volume of their own.

The first casualties, however, came not through enemy action in France or Norway, but as a result of the black-out. Many minor roads still had undefined footpaths beside them and there were numerous accidents.

Some 180 local men were killed in action or died as a direct result of military service, and many more returned home wounded; others survived many dangers and hardships but suffered emotional and psychological damage and subsequently found it difficult to settle back into civilian life. In the town itself air raid warnings had been frequent, particularly during the so-called Midlands Blitz. In early September 1940 the Luftwaffe photographed the town and a month later returned to bomb the premises of the English Electric Company. Another type of aerial incident occurred on 4 July 1944, when Captain Perrin of the USAAF courageously stayed at the controls of his doomed P-51 Mustang, desperately trying to steer the aircraft away from housing as it crashed.

Members of the Stafford Troop of the Staffordshire Yeomanry (The Queen's Own Royal Regiment, or QORR) fought in the North Africa campaign, and later played a crucial role in the D-Day landings on Sword Beach. Both the QORR and the Stafford Battery earned many battle honours during the liberation of Europe, while members of 293 (Stafford) Company of the Royal Engineers served both at home and abroad, fighting in France and Belgium with the British Expeditionary Force (BEF) in 1940. The Stafford Company was a sapper unit attached to the Guards Armoured Division, and its men were to serve alongside the Guards throughout the north-west Europe campaign of 1944–45.

The Stafford Corporation Arms. (Reproduced by courtesy of Stafford Borough Council)

The stories of many individuals are recorded within these pages; others have sadly been lost for ever. This volume is intended to serve as a tribute to all who served their country and the cause of freedom.

Chapter One

Unknown Warriors

'This is a war of unknown warriors'

Winston Churchill

Throughout the late 1930s England geared itself up for what seemed to be an inevitable war with Germany. Following two decades of cutbacks, particularly in the RAF, all branches of the Armed Services were weakened and in desperate need of modernisation. The Royal Air Force Volunteer Reserve (RAFVR) was formed in 1937 to supplement the RAF's trained pilots and aircrew, while the Army and Royal Navy went through a similar expansion programme, putting their reserve forces on a war footing. In May 1939 Britain introduced the Military Training Act, under which every man between the ages of 20 and 22 could be subject to six months of military training.

Meanwhile, in response to nationwide appeals for war workers to fight on the Home Front, thousands more men and women came forward to serve in the Air Raid Precautions (ARP), Auxiliary Fire Service (AFS), Home Guard (HG), Fire Guard (FG), Civil Defence (CD), First Aid Nursing Yeomanry (FANY), Voluntary Aid Detachment (VAD), Auxiliary Territorial Service (ATS), Women's Auxiliary Air Force (WAAF), Women's Royal Navy Service (WRENS) and in the Land Army. As Winston Churchill himself later remarked on the new age of warfare:

> The whole warring nations are engaged, not only soldiers but the entire population, men, women and children. The fronts are everywhere. The trenches are dug in the towns and streets. Every village is fortified. Every road is barred. The front line runs through the factories. The workmen are soldiers with different weapons – but the same courage.

The possible nature of the forthcoming war with Germany had already been brought home by the events of the Spanish Civil War, where for the first time civilians had been seen as legitimate targets for bombing. The ARP was formed to help counter this new but very real threat.

The British feared gas attacks too, and by late October 1938 some

Members of Stafford's Civil Defence Volunteers, c. 1940.

19,745 civilian gas masks had already been issued in Stafford, while another 9,500 were stock-piled at The Beeches on the Stone road ready for distribution. One Staffordian recalled his local air raid warden, Mr Alf Gibbons of 102 Sandon Road, visiting his parents' house to 'fit' them for their gas masks, which they collected a few days later from a house in Bath Street opposite the old police station:

> Everyone had to carry their gas masks all the time, to work during the day and even to the cinema and dances at night. Schoolchildren wore their gas masks during some lessons too, in order to make sure they put them on properly.
>
> The masks were issued with a small cardboard box which was worn around the neck on a piece of string. The boxes didn't last long and were replaced by biscuit tins and containers made with recycled leather. More fashionable containers were produced by Lotus Shoes as a side-line.

Gas masks for the under-twos had yet to be issued in any number. These, like the helmets designed for hospital patients, had to be hand-pumped to maintain the flow of filtered air.

In November 1938 the county's ARP plans were announced. Every area had its own control centre and each street its warden. The Stafford volunteers formed part of 8 Midlands Division, ARP. Mr T. Broughton Nowell, the town clerk, acted as the Warden Controller. The control centre, which was linked by telephone to a network of twenty-five warden posts strategically positioned around the town, was up and running by mid-May 1939. It was manned in shifts to provide a 24-hour service to cover any emergency.

Senior schoolboys were appointed as runners to carry messages in the event of the loss of telephone communications. They were supplied with bicycles after an appeal was made by the town clerk for the loan of one hundred of them for the duration of hostilities.

The town was divided into eleven sectors with every street having its own reference, while area commanders were people who were well known in the local community.

The Stafford Sectors

Sector 1:	Holmcroft
Sector 2:	Stafford Common
Sector 3:	Oxford Gardens/Browning Street
Sector 4:	Castletown and Doxey
Sector 5:	Riverway and Littleworth
Sector 6:	County Road/Union Street
Sector 7:	Albion Place/Foregate Street
Sector 8:	Forebridge
Sector 9:	Wolverhampton Road from the railway bridge to Burton Manor
Sector 10:	Lichfield Road from St Leonards Street to the borough boundary
Sector 11:	Rising Brook/Royal Oak to the borough boundary

Mobilised for war on 1 September 1939, the Stafford ARP was fully operational by early October, although with thirty-seven posts instead of the projected twenty-five, while a decontamination centre had been established at the Corporation's Lammascote Road Depot.

In response to a call for 'the construction of defence works, such as digging trenches and erecting obstacles designed to hamper enemy landings', volunteers from the English Electric Company joined other locals in filling sandbags to protect public buildings such as the District Hospital and adjoining Nurses Homes. Among those helping out was George Crewe:

> It was a very sunny morning and we were all feeling the heat. I remember we stopped for a cuppa. 'Chillo', one of the older men on the gang, was sitting opposite me and asked me if I thought that we would go to war. I said that I hoped not. Chillo said he thought we were closer to war than we were to lunch-break.

Stafford at War

The date was 1 September 1939. Only a few hours later news would come through of Germany's invasion of Poland. There followed an ultimatum from the British government to Adolf Hitler, which expired at 1100 hours on 3 September. The *Staffordshire Advertiser* of 8 September carried an outline of the events leading up to the declaration of war, under the heading 'A Momentous Week':

> As these words are written, there is drawing to a close what must be one of the most momentous weeks in the history of Britain – a week which has seen the commencement, for the second time, of a war with Germany. Britain united as never before, unanimously supported by her vast Empire, has joined forces with her mighty ally France in going to the aid of Poland, the latest victim of a ruthless Nazi Germany which, with all the terrible means at its command, is seeking to wipe her from the map.

Germany failed to respond to the British ultimatum and consequently the Prime Minister, Neville Chamberlain, addressed the nation at 11.15 am on the 3rd, announcing that no such undertaking had been made and that 'consequently we are at war with Germany'.

On the outbreak of hostilities Stafford, which lay close to the heart of the industrial West Midlands, still lacked adequate air raid shelters, despite the fact that as early as October 1938 Major Vernon had given a public lecture stressing their need. One company, however, was doing its best to offer Staffordians some protection. Haywoods of Stafford was busy manufacturing its own type of shelter, a steel and sand bag construction, for sale locally. Meanwhile, Stafford's schools had been provided with slit-trenches, and these would be made available to the public out of school hours.

A survey of all the town's basements was conducted with a view to creating public shelters in some of them; the Shirehall's could accommodate between 150 and 200 people. Meanwhile plans were being made to construct a trench behind the Library and to adapt a basement in the nearby brewery yard.

By 9 July 1940, the eve of the Battle of Britain, the situation in Stafford had not yet been resolved and so a panel of local architects and engineers was formed to give advice on how to strengthen cellars.

One of the more mundane tasks of the ARP wardens, and the one for which they are best known, was to patrol the streets at night checking for any chinks of light that might prove an aid to German bombers. ARP notices and, from 3 September 1939, blackout times were to become a regular feature on bill-boards and in the press.

IMPORTANT NOTICE

BOROUGH OF STAFFORD

AIR RAID PRECAUTIONS
Night of July 13th/14th, 1939

In connection with Royal Air Force exercises on July 13th and 14th it is desired to secure that no lights are visible from the air between midnight and 4 a.m. in the morning of July 14th.

The darkening of areas exposed to air attack may be expected to be an essential feature of the defence of this country in time of war, and useful information on the best means of effecting this may be derived from the present Exercise.

HOUSEHOLDERS AND ALL OTHER OCCUPIERS OF PREMISES ARE ACCORDINGLY ASKED TO ASSIST BY ENSURING THAT LIGHTS IN THEIR PREMISES ARE EXTINGUISHED, OR SCREENED BY DARK CURTAINS OR BLINDS, BETWEEN MIDNIGHT AND 4 A.M. IN THE MORNING OF JULY 14TH. IT IS PARTICULARLY DESIRABLE THAT EXTERNAL LIGHTS AND OTHER LIGHTS DIRECTLY VISIBLE FROM THE SKY SHOULD BE EXTINGUISHED OR SCREENED.

As lighting in streets will be restricted, vehicles should, so far as possible, keep off the roads during the darkened period.

It is emphasized that there is no intention, in connection with the "Blackout," of cutting off lighting or power supplies at the mains.

T. BROUGHTON NOWELL,
Town Clerk.

Notification in the press of an ARP exercise held in conjunction with the RAF to check the town's blackout precautions.

Members of Stafford's ARP parade for inspection by the Earl of Harroby in 1939.

Fines of up to £100 or a maximum three-month prison sentence could be incurred by anyone who was found showing a light. The *Stafford Chronicle* of 28 December 1940 carried details of a hearing into a breach of the regulations at Lotus Shoes, where thirty windows were found to show a 'dark green light' visible at 20 or 30 yards, while one was totally uncovered. Ironically the lights were only seen because workmen were busy installing blackout material for the factory's 1,000 windows, which covered some 44,000 square feet. Despite the mitigating circumstance, Mr F.M. Bostock, whose family owned Lotus Shoes, was fined £28 and the company £13.

Advertisement for blackout materials. Fines of up to £100 were imposed on anyone who failed to observe the restrictions.

From 1940 'Summertime' began in February in order to maximise daylight working hours, while the summer months saw 'Double Summertime' hours observed. Meanwhile car headlights and cycle lights had to be fitted with special 'blinkers' which restricted their usefulness.

Stafford's ARP wardens were thrown into turmoil in February 1943 with the appointment of a conscientious objector to the post of ARP Organiser and Training Officer. Four of the five Warden Groups held protest meetings, while the town's senior wardens threatened to resign. In the event the Corporation was forced to back down and terminate the appointment.

The blackout restrictions were not lifted until October 1944, but even then it was little more than a slackening of the regulations.

Fire Fighting

Prior to the formation of the National Fire Service (NFS) in August 1941, Stafford was served by its own Volunteer Fire Brigade (established in 1877). During the years leading up to the Second World War there had been a call for volunteers to help form the Auxiliary Fire Service

(AFS), and by 1939 it had an estimated 120,000 members nationwide. Stafford and most of the Staffordshire Service formed part of Fire Force Area 25 of the NFS.

In February 1938 the Stafford contingent received a new Dennis trailer pump, which was first used 'in anger' to put out a fire that nearly destroyed the Izaak Walton Cottage at Shallowford only a few months later. Sometimes the auxiliaries used their own cars to reach the scene of an emergency, often heavily laden with a complement of firemen, plus a ladder and length of hose.

A new Leyland-built engine was purchased in May, at a cost of £1,652 10s, and presented to the Stafford Fire Brigade on New Year's Day 1940. This Leyland 50 'Hippo' class engine was christened *Eveline* after the Mayoress, Mrs Eveline Joynes. *Eveline* and her crew served in both Coventry and Birmingham from November 1940, while Lieutenant Ernest Haywood (junior) and Lieutenant Hill commanded Stafford detachments seconded to Liverpool and Manchester. Former Leading Firewoman Miss Margaret Pye later recalled 'the men returning from these duties looking terribly tired and devastated by the horrors they had witnessed'.

Members of Stafford's Auxiliary Fire Service, 1939.

The town had recently raised funds (£320 11s 6d by 5 November) for two mobile canteens, which were duly dispatched to Coventry the morning after the city suffered its first air raid. The staff worked for 48 hours without relief, and the comment was made that: 'If these mobile canteens never did another job of work they will have fully justified the money spent upon them by the invaluable help they have been able to give to the stricken people of Coventry.' Stafford would also make a gift to the people of Coventry of £1,000 from the Mayor's Bombed Areas Fund.

Detachments from the Stafford Fire Brigade also went further afield, to London and to many of Britain's major ports. One local fireman, Leslie Haywood, was transferred to Lewisham where he served throughout the Blitz. He narrowly escaped death when bombs destroyed the fire station just moments after he had driven the lead engine out on to the street; the second engine and its crew caught the full blast.

On 18 December 1940 the Duke of Kent made a tour of Stafford, inspecting the Stafford Fire Brigade in the town's Market Square. Chief Officer Ernest Haywood had the honour of presenting the fire crews, who included Ernest Haywood (junior), then a second officer. 'His Royal Highness then proceeded to inspect the detachments of various services, pausing to chat with the members.' These members included the town's Home Guard, Civil Defence and British Red Cross representatives. The duke later moved on to the English Electric Company, where he inspected an honour-guard of the factory's Home Guard before meeting senior managers and touring the factory.

The Stafford Fire Brigade attended countless incidents throughout the war, but undoubtedly one of the biggest was the explosion of the bomb dump at the Fauld, or 21 RAF Maintenance Unit (21 MU), at 11.11 hours on 27 November 1944. This massive explosion, which rocked the area around Uttoxeter for miles, happened when the greater part of 4,000 tons of high explosives stored in a former gypsum mine detonated. Where once a hill and farmhouses had stood, there was now an enormous crater, some 600 yards long and 350 yards wide.

As well as extinguishing the resulting blaze, the firemen also had to deal with ignited incendiary bombs and assist with an underground search of the partly collapsed tunnels in the former mine. They also had the gruesome task of helping to locate the remains of the sixty casualties, before they were relieved by the rescue teams of the North Midland Coal Owners Company.

The Local Defence Volunteers

Formed on 14 May 1940, the Local Defence Volunteers (LDV) force was made up of people from all walks of life, including those in reserved occupations and those who were ineligible for military service through age or infirmity. On 28 July that year Winston Churchill renamed this force the Home Guard. Initially, the men paraded with anything that could be considered a lethal weapon. Despite their sometimes comical and less-than-military appearance, all these volunteers were ready and willing to defend their country in the event of an invasion, a threat that was all too real throughout 1940.

F Company, Stafford Home Guard, c. 1942.

The likelihood of an imminent invasion was brought into sharper focus on 22 June 1940, when every household in Stafford received a Ministry of Information flier entitled 'What to do if an Invasion Comes'. Many thought the leaflet should have been called 'When the Invasion Comes'.

The men of the Stafford Home Guard used the rifle ranges at Broad Eye and the larger Cannock Chase ranges. Each company, however, had its own drill hall and parade ground:

Company	Drill Hall	Parade Ground
HQ Company	Bailey Street Drill Hall	Barrack Square Battalion HQ
A Company	Memorial Hall, Church Eaton	Lockett's Field Church
B Company	Baswich House	Baswich School Field
C Company	Friar's Cottage	Universal Grinding Wheel Co. Sports Field
D Company	English Electric Co. Works	English Electric Co. Sports Field
E Company	Rowley Street School	Stafford Common
F Company	Newport Road Drill Hall	King Edward VI Grammar School Field
G Company	Rugeley Drill Hall	Grammar School Field, Rugeley
H Company	Armitage Brickworks	Cathy's Field, Armitage

Meanwhile, the 13th Independent Platoon of the Nottinghamshire (Post Office) Regiment, otherwise known as the Stafford PO Platoon, shared facilities with other units including Stafford's C Company.

From 18 April 1942 the 1/Cadet (Stafford Grammar School) Battalion and 2/Cadet (Stafford) Battalion of the North Staffordshire Regiment became affiliated to the Stafford Home Guard.

The Stafford Home Guard's early duties included guarding local RAF bases, but they were stood down from this task following the formation of the RAF Regiment on 1 February 1942. Later in the war C Company was given the job of testing RAF Seighford's defences.

Concrete gun-emplacements known as pill-boxes were constructed alongside waterways and roads, and at vital crossroads and bridges, in an effort to hamper any invasion force. The Radford Bank pill-box, the last to survive, was only demolished recently to make way for housing. Manned by Bren-gunners from B Company, this pill-box was adjacent to the former Radford Wharf and had a commanding view of the two bridges crossing the River Penk and the Staffordshire & Worcestershire Canal, and was further protected by the marshy ground beyond. It would have been able to provide concentrated fire over the road, river and canal.

Members of the Home Guard were frequently called upon to take over the normal duties of the Regular Army, including protecting government buildings and establishments, guarding PoWs, acting as military escorts and dealing with reports of enemy paratroopers or aircrew who had been forced to bale out. In 1944, during training for the Arnhem operations, members of D Company took on Polish paratroopers, 'fighting' house-clearance operations in derelict buildings along Chell Road.

Membership of the Home Guard was not undertaken lightly. Many men already worked a 12-hour day, seven days a week, with only one weekend off a month. After work they reported for duty at 20.00 hours, and might not stand down again until 08.00 hours the following morning. Under these circumstances, it seems rather unfair that failure to attend parade resulted in a fine of up to two weeks' wages.

On 1 November 1944, with the counter-invasion of Europe well under way, the Home Guard was finally ordered to stand down. Although it had never been called upon to engage the enemy en masse, many Home Guardsmen had lost their lives in training accidents and air raids, or simply through the hardships of war. Without the help of the tens of thousands of ordinary individuals who gave up their time to protect the Home Front, Britain simply would not have had the manpower to protect her own shores and her interests across the British Empire and beyond.

Chapter Two

Stafford Industry Gears up for War

During the years leading up to the outbreak of the Second World War Britain underwent a period of rearmament in an effort to catch up with Nazi Germany, which had been secretly building up its armed forces in direct contravention of the Treaty of Versailles. Among the firms who began to devote themselves to war work during this period was the English Electric Company, the Stafford factory receiving its first war order as early as 1938.

Among their special commissions were degaussing generators for exploding enemy mines, along with submarine propulsion units and aircraft instruments and valves, as well as parts for hand grenades and other ordnance. The demand was huge. On 25 July 1940, for example, the factory received an order for a million components for Mills bombs, and many more similar orders followed. On 15 January 1941 staff were instructed to supply 14,000 generators, 8,000 speed indicators and 2 million mortar fins, and on 16 July 1941 received an order for 135,000 radio transformers.

The Stafford factory also manufactured a number of different types of tank, including the Covenantor (of which 1,771 were made), the Centaur and the Comet,

Sir George Nelson, Director of the English Electric Company.

as well as producing the turrets for the new Cromwell tank. These armoured vehicles were regularly put through their paces on the firm's testing grounds on Cannock Chase. The Covenantor had thin armour, a fairly ineffective gun and a riveted turret, and consequently was

11

A Comet tank on the production line at the English Electric Company, Stafford.

unpopular with its crews. Although it was in production by 1940, this type of tank could not be used in the North Africa campaign because its Meadows engine was prone to overheating.

The new Cromwell tanks began rolling off the production line in 1943, but it was nearly a year before they were considered battle-ready. Powered by a Rolls-Royce Meteor engine and armed with either a 95mm gun or the British 75mm gun, the Cromwell carried heavier armour than the American Sherman, which had earned itself the unpleasant nickname the 'Tommy Cooker' because of its propensity to

A Cromwell tank on the tank testing grounds at Cannock Chase.

catch fire. Combining reliability, a high maximum speed, a useful general-purpose gun, reasonable armour and a low silhouette, the Cromwell was second only in importance to the more famous Churchill as the mainstay of the 21st Army Group. Like most tanks, however, it only enjoyed a brief period of superiority and was soon outclassed in every department.

On D-Day, 6 June 1944, Cromwell tanks with chain flails on the front were sent in ahead of the advancing troops to help clear the beaches of mines. These tanks, which were at least partly manufactured at Stafford, were only to see active service in north-west Europe, being used alongside the Comet, a type which was to play a major part in the crossing of the Rhine.

The importance of the Stafford factory was reflected in the numbers of VIP visitors during the war years. General Charles de Gaulle rode in a Covenantor on the Cannock Chase testing grounds on 21 October 1941, while King George VI and Queen Elizabeth visited the Stafford site on 26 February 1942. On 18 February 1944 the crew of HM Submarine *Visigoth* were welcomed as guests of honour at the factory as part of an adoption process. Launched on 30 November 1943, this submarine survived the latter phase of the Mediterranean campaign.

On 26 February 1942 King George VI and Queen Elizabeth made an official visit to the English Electric Company, in the course of which they toured the Lichfield Road works and saw the tank testing grounds on nearby Cannock Chase.

General de Gaulle shaking hands with one of the factory's Home Guard members at the English Electric Company.

Stafford Industry Gears up for War

Earlier, back in 1941, workers at the Stafford factory had purchased bonds to the value of £24,000 for the purchase of a motor torpedo boat. They were to play an important part in the town's saving campaign, investing £1,000,000 by early December 1944.

Meanwhile, Messrs W.H. Dorman & Company stepped up the production of diesel engines at their Foregate factory, which also produced control gear used in Navy torpedoes and the Flextel couplings used in the 'Pluto' petrol pipeline laid under the Channel to supply the Allies after the D-Day landings. Similarly, the Universal Grinding Wheel Company increased its production of grinding-wheels. As the UK's only producer of aluminium powder, which was used for fine polishing, the factory became a prime target for enemy bombers. Elsewhere in the town Lotus produced boots and shoes as well as becoming involved in the munitions industry, manufacturing nose-caps for the 20mm armour-piercing shells used in RAF cannon. Meanwhile, a new railway line was built off the Norton Bridge–Stone line to serve the Royal Ordnance factory at nearby Swynnerton.

All of Stafford's major industries supplied munitions in some form or another, or did special war work, while many men and women worked long shifts in the factories and then raced off home to change ready for fire-watching or other duties with the Civil Defence, Home Guard or ARP. Larger factories, including English Electric, Universal Grinding and British Reinforced Concrete, which manufactured all manner of shelters and gun emplacements and worked on the Mulberry floating docks, had their own ARP, Home Guard and fire brigade.

Fire-watchers were stationed all around the town, taking advantage of various landmarks such as Stafford Castle, while anti-aircraft gun positions were located between the castle and the town.

Brass ashtrays like this one were made by English Electric and sold to raise funds for the crew of HM Submarine Visigoth.

Chapter Three

Warning Sirens

The drone of German bombers overhead was a familiar sound in the West Midlands, particularly during the Blitz. Stragglers from the Merseyside raids, which began on 9 August 1940 and had numbered some 300 individual attacks by mid-December, might easily venture as far west as Staffordshire, selecting industrial targets of opportunity.

Unfortunately for Stafford, the railway network that converged on the town, along with the rivers Sow and Trent and the Shropshire Union and Trent & Mersey canals, all proved useful navigation aids to the enemy. Furthermore, the presence of heavy industry there, including English Electric, Bagnalls, Dorman Diesels, BRC and Universal Grinding, along with the RAF's 16 Maintenance Unit, made the town a prime target.

On 3 September 1940, on the first anniversary of the outbreak of war, a Junkers Ju 88 A-1 photo-reconnaissance aircraft flew at high altitude over Stafford, capturing images of the town and its industrial complexes. The photographs, which survived the war and are now housed at Keele, may have been used in the briefing of Luftwaffe aircrews. One month later, on 9 October, a second German medium bomber, having slipped through 12 Group's airspace, flew over the town.

The air was filled with the piercing whine of air raid sirens, soon followed by the distant noise of an aircraft. While many townsfolk thought it was just another drill, others were confused and didn't know what to do. Searching the sky for reassurance, all eyes focused on a 'British bomber' that could be seen moving slowly across the distant horizon. A fighter followed it and all seemed well, until the gunners at Universal Grinding suddenly opened fire on the enemy aircraft, which flew on to its selected target undeterred.

Schoolgirls at nearby Riverway sat anxiously in their shelter. One of their teachers ventured out to see what was happening, only to return hurriedly a few moments later, pale and trembling, having just witnessed a string of bombs exploding only a few hundred yards away.

Warning Sirens

That evening, Wednesday, 9 October 1940, a German propaganda broadcast carried the news that:

A German bomber this morning dived from a low altitude in a bold attack on an industrial works near Stafford. Heavy bombs screamed down into the main works and into annexes with tremendous explosive force. The extensive building was blown into the air by the force of the explosion.

Meanwhile, details of the raid were reported in the pages of the *Stafford Chronicle* on 12 October under the heading 'Midlands Town's First Raid', which was deliberately vague so as not to positively identify Stafford as the Luftwaffe's target. The report read:

When a Midland town had its first air raid a lone German two-engined medium bomber dived from the clouds and circled about for some time and dropped four high explosive bombs, one of which failed to explode. It was dug up by a military bomb disposal unit and taken to one of the holes made by one of the other bombs on wasteland some distance away, and detonated.

Some damage was caused to one building, and one or two girls were slightly injured by splinters of glass. Only one was taken to hospital, and after treatment she was allowed to go home.

A man who saw the attack from an office window in the town said the bomber suddenly dived out of a bank of clouds steeply to a very low level before releasing its bombs. The plane then straightened out and flew away with two English fighters, who had apparently spotted him when he made his dive, on its tail.

Some houses [eleven] had their windows blown out by the blast, and at a public baths several panes were dislodged. No extensive damage to household properties, however, was caused.

Many people were shopping in the town when the bombs exploded and they immediately hurried for cover in shelters or in shops. Heavy traffic continued on its way.

Anecdotal evidence suggests there was at least one further raid on Stafford, during which a fighter fended off a bomber that was apparently targeting 16 MU. Spent machine-gun cartridges were picked up at the north end of Oxford Gardens following this unsuccessful combat. Another report placed a similar – possibly the same – brush with the enemy over Tixall Road, while a third person reported machine-gun fire over Corporation Street. In both instances spent bullet cases are believed to have been recovered somewhere towards 16 MU.

Mike Shelley recalled hearing an explosion near 16 MU, and subsequently the family's lodger, a serviceman working at the RAF camp, brought home a piece of shrapnel which he mounted on a wooden plinth, with a label giving details of the raid.

The ever-present threat of bombing was generally faced with unfailing humour, as illustrated by a joke which appeared in the *Stafford Chronicle* in January 1941:

> The roof-spotter was excited.
> 'There's a bomb falling,' he telegraphed down. 'It's coming so near I could catch it.'
> A moment later there was a terrific explosion.
> His colleagues below snapped one word into the telephone: 'Butter-fingers.'

The war was, however, a deadly serious business and an article published in the *Stafford Chronicle* in November 1940 reported without comment the purchase of a hundred shrouds to be used in the event of Stafford suffering mass casualties.

An ARP log kept by local wardens confirms the frequency of Stafford's air raid alerts, of which there were 284 in the period from 1939 to 1944. There were different levels of readiness depending on the perceived threat, with each level having its own designated colour. These ranged from 'raid imminent'(Red) to the 'all clear' (White). The first recorded alert occurred at 03.48 hours on 6 December 1939, but thankfully the night proved uneventful and the 'all clear' sounded at 04.13 hours.

The fall of France in 1940 had given the Luftwaffe access to airfields that brought its aircraft within easy striking distance of Britain and by 10 July, the first day of the Battle of Britain, Goering was already launching air raids on our shores. But the RAF would not give in, and by 15 September its pilots had proved they had the upper hand and the Luftwaffe eventually turned to night raids. This resulted in the London Blitz, and countless raids on ports and industrial targets.

Alerts in Stafford became more frequent during the second half of the year, reflecting the build-up to the so-called Midlands Blitz, which saw frequent raids on Birmingham, Walsall, Wolverhampton, Stoke-on-Trent and Coventry. In total, Stafford's alerts in 1940 may be summarised as follows: June (3), July (7), August (26), September (28), October (52), November (56), December (33). As well as targeting heavy industry, the Luftwaffe also turned its attention to the rural economy, dropping incendiaries on crops in the fields. On 19 August

Warning Sirens

1940 this message was received from Rugeley ARP control centre:

1) All wardens to be on alert for fires in ripening crops. Beating to be employed where possible, pending arrival of Fire Parties.

2) All wardens to be cautioned that delayed-action bombs are being used. Any unexploded bombs are to be regarded with utmost suspicion and cordoned till arrival of military authorities.

3) No member of the public to be allowed to collect or retain any parts of bombs or unexploded bombs. Public to be warned of danger of picking up unexploded bombs whether HE or incendiary.

On 6 September there were two Red Alerts, and a string of bombs was dropped close to the county town:

Air Raid Warning	Red	21.08 hours
	White	23.00 hours
	Red	23.52 hours
	White	03.33 hours

Enquiry from Control. Bombs believed to have dropped in a line between Dunstan and Coppenhall. Reported six explosions at 02.38 hours between this post and the Potteries, probably Stone.

The next mention of bombs dropping close to the county town came on 22 October 1940:

Air Raid Message	Purple	19.27 hours
	Red	19.31 hours
	White	22.49 hours

One incendiary bomb dropped at the north-west of the district in a field occupied by Mr Sumner (next to the field numbered 354 on the Ordnance Survey map) at 22.20 hours.

The bomb was extinguished by a Mr Booth, a member of the Home Guard; the parts were taken by Mr Taylor who has handed them to the Dunstan Police officers.

Adverse weather conditions in early 1941 meant fewer penetrating air raids across the West Midlands, while the last phases of the Midlands Blitz saw two further raids on Coventry and one on Birmingham. Alerts in Stafford in 1941 were as follows: January (12), February (0), March (6), April (7), May (10), June (6), July (3), August (1), September (20), October (3), November (1), December (1).

One raid for which we have details took place on 11 March 1941:

11 March 1941

Wardens arrived for duty as bombs dropped 21.12 hours.

Air Raid message Red at 21.25 hours.

Message to Control at 21.25 hours reporting HE bombs dropped at approx 21.12 hours [in the] direction [of] Bradley and also in a direction between Coppenhall and Stafford Castle.

Air Raid message White at 2400 hours.

By 1942 there were fewer alerts in Stafford, with 1 in January, 6 in July and 2 in August, for example, while the following year only two alerts were recorded, one each in March and April. In 1944 there were three pre-D-Day air raid alerts, two in January and the third in April. Both the January alerts were part of a series of exercises aimed at testing the local Civil Defence, with residents being warned to expect the use of CS gas and to have their gas masks ready for immediate use.

Chapter Four

On Ration

In November 1936 the Board of Trade established a Department of Food, the role of which was to make preparations for food rationing in the event of war. Prices would be fixed by the government, thus reducing the profiteering and escalating price rises seen under the free market during the First World War.

In the pre-war years Britain imported annually some 55 million tons of food and raw materials, including oil, rubber, steel and timber. Much of this came across the Atlantic Ocean from the USA and Canada, and some from other parts of the Empire and the colonies. To maintain this flow of goods, even in the early days of the war, the Merchant Navy had to run the gauntlet of the Kriegsmarine, and in particular the German U-boats. This so-called Battle of the Atlantic was not won until late 1943, and in all some 2,500 vessels and their crews were lost. As Churchill famously remarked: 'The only thing that ever really frightened me during the war was the U-boat peril.' Of course, in the immediate pre-war years the Department of Trade had stockpiled non-perishable food items, but these supplies were finite and if Britain were to survive, the ships had to get through.

The answer lay in rationing supplies. Petrol rationing was introduced in September 1939, and ration books were issued to all householders in October. Measures were introduced to limit the sale of bacon, butter and sugar from 8 January 1940, and meat rationing was introduced on 11 March; from June 1940 customers had to be registered with a butcher in order for their coupons to be accepted. The supply and use of coupons was very strictly monitored in order to prevent anyone getting more than their fair share, with adults limited to 16 points per month. There were, however, always some who found ways to beat the system.

As part of the National Economy Campaign, the County Education Committee in Stafford organised short courses entitled 'Food Economy in War Time'. These were held throughout the latter part of May 1940 at the Senior Girls' School, Riverway, Rowley Street Library, the Public Library, and at the Electricity Showrooms on Greengate Street.

An advertisement for the National Food Campaign, May 1940.

All imported goods were scarce, but not all commodities were rationed from the outset: tea and margarine, for example, were only added to the list in July 1940. Jam went on ration from March 1941 and cheese two months later, eggs being added in June. Dried fruit and rice were only subject to rationing from January 1942, and tinned tomatoes and peas a month later. Meanwhile, 26 July that year saw the introduction of rationing for sweets and chocolate, with biscuits following suit a month later.

A typical adult's weekly ration was as follows:

Meat	6 oz or 150 grams
Eggs	1
Butter/margarine/lard	4 oz or 100 grams
Cheese	4 oz or 100 grams
Bacon	4 oz or 100 grams
Sugar	8 oz or 200 grams
Tea	2 oz or 50 grams
Sweets	2 oz or 50 grams

Young children, adolescents and pregnant women were allowed additional rations, which included cod liver oil and orange juice, along with extra milk and vitamins.

On Ration

Stafford's St John's Market was taken over by the government and became the town's food depot, supplies being distributed to local shops from this central point. Meanwhile, a mutual assistance scheme was established between Stafford and several other towns in order to safeguard the distribution of food in the event of air raid damage, the people of Birmingham, Coventry and Stoke-on-Trent being among the beneficiaries.

The first winter of the war was exceptionally cold. Coal had already been rationed owing to the rising demands from heavy industry, but further problems occurred as most of the country was snowbound and suppliers could not get through. Children and pensioners queued in the snow outside the town's gas works on Chell Road to buy coke to help supplement their meagre ration.

Despite the large numbers of Staffordians who were drafted into the Services, the town's population expanded by one-third during the war, rising from 31,000 to about 41,000; despite this, food and other allocations remained at pre-war levels.

The 'Dig for Victory' Campaign

Although they were scarce in the shops, vegetables were not rationed. As part of the national 'Dig for Victory' campaign, flowerbeds and lawns were turned into vegetable patches. Meanwhile, allotment and horticultural committees were set up to make the best use of available land, which included school playing fields and other publicly owned plots, much of which was put under the plough.

Many farm labourers had been conscripted into the Services and their places were taken by ladies from the Women's Land Army (WLA) and the Timber Corps. Many of the local girls trained at Rodbaston College and worked a 48-hour week for 28s; those under 18 received 22s 6d.

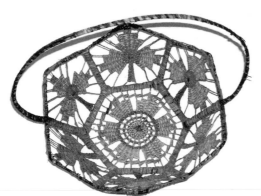

This straw basket was handmade by an Italian prisoner from the Hopton Camp and given to his farmer host at Weston Bank.

Stafford at War

From October 1942 Italian PoWs were granted free licence to work on local farms, as long as they returned to camp before their curfew. Many worked alongside WLA girls and countless friendships were formed. Schoolchildren helped too, especially during the summer holidays and at weekends. The county's first school camp was established at Lower Cowley Farm, Gnosall, and was attended by twenty-four pupils. They looked after poultry and mucked out the cattle before helping out with the potato harvest. One former schoolboy recalled that patriotism wasn't the only reason for volunteering to help bring in the harvest:

> It was about 1943 or '44 that we realised we could get out of school by going potato-picking. We would gather early in the morning for the tractor and flat-topped trailer to pick us up, about twenty of us in all, most about 12 or 13 years of age but some were younger.
>
> As I remember those autumn mornings always seemed to be cold, damp and foggy as we huddled together wearing our heavy coats, balaclavas and fingerless gloves. We all scrambled up on to the trailer clutching a bag full of snap [food]. Most of us had sandwiches, usually spread with homemade jam. Halfway through the morning the farmer would bring us a bucket of cocoa. I swear it was made from builder's sand as it tasted horrible but it was all we had. I forget how much we were paid but it wasn't much.

Meanwhile, children at one local school pickled and bottled peas, beans, carrots and onions. They also collected dandelion and burdock leaves and roots, belladonna leaves and foxgloves, and harvested nettles for food colouring. They picked blackberries too, while acorns and chestnuts were gathered to feed pigs, which were also given swill made from kitchen scraps collected daily at the Corporation Depot. During the summer holidays in 1941 pupils from the King Edward VI Grammar School even spent a month working at the Ministry of Supply's Home Grown Timber Production Depot at the Derwent Valley Camp.

Poachers managed to do good business throughout the war years. Rabbits were wild and of course unregistered. Both the government and farmers were anxious to cut down their population because of the damage they did to the crops. Each rabbit would sell for 1s 8d. A number of tragedies occurred, including one at a farm near Stafford where a young boy had been out shooting rabbits with his father's shotgun. While cleaning the gun in the kitchen, he accidentally caught the trigger and shot his mother at point-blank range. Distraught, the boy ran out into the yard where a second shot soon rang out.

On Ration

Clothing was not put on ration until 1 June 1941, while soap was added to the list in February 1942. Clothing was sold on a points system, with utility clothing replacing fashionable items. Cheap materials were utilised where possible and designs used the most economical cuts. Pleats were banned and even the number of pockets was regulated. Everyone was allowed 66 points per year. The 'Make Do and Mend' campaign encouraged people to patch worn clothing and have old shoes repaired. Second-hand items, however, were not covered by the points system.

Pre-war luxuries such as silk and nylon became virtually impossible to obtain (at least until the Americans entered the war in late 1941) as they were reserved for the manufacture of parachutes and barrage balloons.

Everyone, including schoolchildren, helped with the salvage programme. Bones, for example, were collected, rendered down and used to make nitro-glycerin, soap, glue, feeding flour for cattle, and fertilisers. All scrap metal, including iron railings and old pots and pans, was collected for recycling. As it turned out, though, much of the iron collected was too badly rusted to use and ended up being dumped in the North Sea. Copper, zinc, lead, aluminium and bronze, however, were all salvaged and used in the production of tanks, aircraft and munitions. Schools collected rags to be turned into anything from blankets and uniforms through to linen maps or roofing felt for bombed-out houses. Recycled cotton was used to make the large white pound notes.

Comparison chart for Stafford's Salvage Campaign, June 1940		
	Population	Salvage
Stafford	32,190	£680
Crewe	45,900	£183
Salford	199,400	£1,009
Stoke	272,100	£1,440

Chapter Five

Wartime Entertainment and Fundraising

O n 2 September 1939 an announcement was made banning all public performances because of the threat of bombing. This ban was later reversed, but one of the war's first casualties was the town's annual Pageant and Carnival, held annually to raise funds for Stafford District Hospital. The reasons given were that 'the restrictions on the use of paper for decorations, together with intensified war production, which calls on us all to work long hours and weekends, do not lend themselves to the preparation that is required for such an effort'.

STAFFORD'S "STIRLING" EFFORT

" The conditions to which the great centres of German war industry, and particu'arly the Ruhr, are being reduced is one of unpara'leled devastation."

The Prime Minister in his address to the United States Congress (Washington, 19-5-43)

★ Your Savings Are Directly Responsible For Britain's Growing Air Might!

IN THIS WEEK PAY YOUR UTMOST TRIBUTE TO THE R.A.F.

Advertisement of the Stafford Local Savings Committee

This was part of the official acknowledgement of Stafford's 'Stirling effort' in Wings for Victory Week, 1943.

"WINGS FOR VICTORY"

STAFFORD

is going to buy

6 STIRLING BOMBERS

for the Victory effort

£250,000

is the cost—you must help.

GIVEN BY :—
STAFFORD RAILWAY PERMANENT BENEFIT BUILDING SOCIETY, 4, Market Sq., Stafford.

An advertisement illustrating Stafford's Wings Week, 1943.

To the People of Stafford

AN APPEAL

I propose to launch an appeal for creating a Central Fund to supply comforts to the men of Stafford serving in all branches of H.M. Forces, and I invite *all* organisations in the town to send a representative to a meeting to be held at 7 p.m. in the Committee Room, Borough Hall, on Wednesday next, November 1st.

At this meeting I am anxious that a strong Committee may be formed and also to launch the appeal for the Fund.

H. JOYNES,
Mayor.

Mayor's Parlour, Stafford.
October 27th, 1939.

Stafford's Comfort Fund was launched on 27 October 1939, and by March 1940 the committee members (pictured below in December 1939) had helped to raise some £2,750 to supply Stafford's servicemen with comfort parcels.

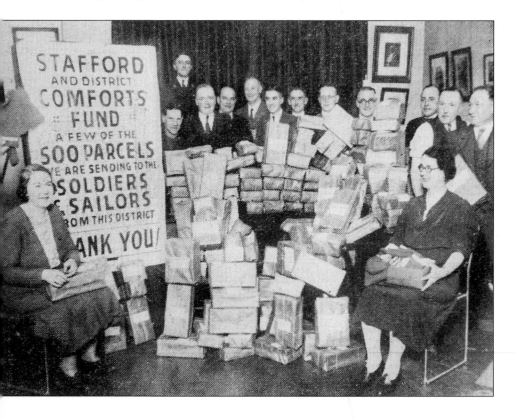

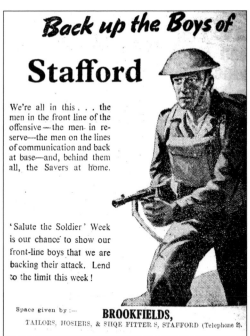

Three advertisements supporting Stafford's Salute the Soldier Week, 13–20 May 1944.

Fundraising became an important part of life in wartime Stafford and as a consequence all types of art, culture and public entertainment positively flourished. There were talks and exhibitions, concerts and dinner-dances, with the town playing host to a variety of Service bands, both British and later American, while the Royal Philharmonic and the Birmingham Philharmonic Orchestras paid several visits. Other methods of fundraising included house-to-house and street collections. Competition was encouraged and the total amounts raised by individual streets and factories were published in the local press. During the war the people of Stafford raised a staggering £6,000,000 in Saving Certificates, Defence Bonds, Savings Deposits, War Bonds, Exchequer Bonds and Savings Bonds.

FIGHTER PILOTS SAY—

WE'VE GOT YOUR NEW PANS!

You know we are as sorry as you are that you can't have that kitchen of yours looking bright and new as you used to. Material for those prized pots and pans goes to provide the equipment for our airmen. The fighter pilot knows this and appreciates your sacrifice. Let us remember the R.A.F. and be grateful.

STAFFORD & STONE
Co-operative
SOCIETY

Press advertisement for the town's salvage campaign.

STAFFORD BOROUGH WAR
SAVINGS COMMITTEE

Congratulations,
Stafford War
Savers

TOTAL NOW
£5,000,000

 KEEP ON SAVING

In early 1945 Stafford broke the £5,000,000 barrier in war savings and bonds.

STAFFORD'S
WAR WEAPONS WEEK
November 2nd – 9th

Support your own Group
SAVINGS KIOSK or Shop

Advertisement for the Victory Drive campaign, 1940.

STAFFORD
WAR WEAPONS WEEK
NOVEMBER 4th—9th
To raise £100,000

and it can be done if we all do our part. £100,000 will pay for 1,000 Machine Guns — and the Army needs them NOW for your defence.

IT MIGHT HAVE BEEN YOURS
Lend your money
AND END THIS SLAUGHTER
—Soon

For the larger investor, National War Bonds are the more appropriate channel, and apart from that duty we feel is an excellent investment.

LEND ALL YOU CAN

Advertisement for War Weapons Week, 1940.

29

Stafford at War

Fund	Dates	Purchase	Target	Donations
Borough Division, Red Cross Flag Day	18/5/40	-	-	£252 8s 3d
Soldiers', Sailors' and Airmen's Flag Day	25/5/40	-	-	£122 13s 9d
Stafford & District Bombed Areas Distress Fund	Oct 1940 –Nov 1940	-	-	£1,000
Mayors Mobile Canteen Fund	5/11/40	Two mobile canteens	-	£320 11s 6d
YMCA War Service Appeal	9/1/41	-	£1,500	-
St Dunstan's War Fund	August 1941	-	-	£108 9s 7d
Stafford & District Bombed Areas Distress Fund	27/9/41	-	-	£1,900
Stafford & District Comforts Funds	24/4/42	-	-	£6,246 2s 0d
British Red Cross and St John's Flag Day	13/5/42	-	-	£350
St Dunstan's War Fund	20–25/8/42	-	-	£142 14s 0d
PoW Appeal	19/12/42	-	-	£452
British Red Cross and St John's Flag Day in aid of the Duke of Gloucester's Fund (PoWs)	15/5/43	-	-	£205 0s 1d
Stafford & District Comforts Funds	8/11/43	-	-	£7,263 8s 6d
Children's Corner (*Stafford Chronicle*) for the British Red Cross PoW Fund	11/12/43	-	-	£106 6s 11½d
Penny a Week Fund	12/12/42– 12/12/43	-	-	£2,130
St Dunstan's War Fund	21/1/44	-	-	£140 7s 10d

Wartime Entertainment and Fundraising

Fund	Dates	Purchase	Target	Donations
British Red Cross and St John's Flag Day in aid of the Duke of Gloucester's Fund (PoWs)	10/6/44	-	-	£540
Air Sea Rescue Craft Fund	-	-	-	£223
Penny a Week Fund	4/12/43–4/11/44	-	-£3,500	
Comforts Fund/Welcome Home Fund	30/6/46	-	-£4,000	

Savings Drive	Date	Aim	Target Amount	Achieved
Stafford Victory Drive	2/11/40 –9/11/40	1,000 Machine Guns	£100,000	£279,095
Tank Week	19/7/41	Ten Tanks	£200,000	£300,000+
Warship Week	8/11/41 –16/11/41	Adopt HM Submarine *Perseus*	£175,000	£307,243
Wings for Victory Week	May 1942	-	£175,000	£300,000
Wings for Victory Week	15/5/43 –22/5/43	Six Stirling Bombers	£250,000	£402,604
Salute the Soldier Week	13/5/44 –20/5/44	Six Base Hospitals	£300,000	£420,192
Thanksgiving Week	3/11/45	-	£300,000	£331,531

Chapter Six

Danger UXB

Tens of thousands of bombs of all descriptions were dropped on Britain during the war. Many failed to detonate due to faulty fuse mechanisms or were fitted with delayed-action fuses. The task of dealing with these unexploded bombs (known as UXBs) fell to a brave few, including Staffordian Stanley Knight.

Born on 12 October 1910, Stanley Knight attended St Leonard's School and later worked for the English Electric Company. Knight joined the Stafford Battery of the Royal Field Artillery (RFA) before enlisting as a sapper in the Royal Engineers (RE). Stanley was selected to go on an officer training course, subsequently passing-out as a second lieutenant. The bombing of London in late 1940 led Stanley to volunteer for one of the newly formed sections hastily established to deal with unexploded German ordnance.

The bomb disposal officers were put under constant strain by the nature of their work and so it was generally accepted that a tour of duty should last no more than six months, after which they were entitled to transfer to other duties. Yet almost to a man, the bomb disposal sections rebuffed this offer of a 'safe' posting.

The year 1940 has been quite rightly described as the 'Heroic Age' of bomb disposal.

Major Stanley Knight MBE served throughout the w.
as a bomb disposal officer with the Royal Engineers.

Danger UXB

It was a period of great individual bravery, when a lack of specialised equipment and practical knowledge led to many officers taking incredible risks on a daily basis, and of course the nature of the work meant that a bomb disposal officer's first mistake was likely to be his last. And the Germans were constantly improving the design of their fuses in order to prevent UXBs from being safely defused, making the job ever more dangerous. Among the many anti-handling devices Stanley and his fellow officers had to face were highly sensitive trembler mechanisms and photoelectric cells. But even basic fuses, especially if they had been damaged on impact, could prove lethal.

For the regulars in the RE's bomb disposal units like Stanley Knight, by then promoted to the rank of temporary major, the end of hostilities brought little change in their daily routine of risking life and limb. The public's impatience for unexploded bombs and minefields to be made safe led to many fatalities, with over 200 officers and men being killed in the line of duty. After the war Stanley worked on a number of long-buried bombs, and in 1946 his gallantry was recognised with the award of the MBE, although he was to work as a bomb disposal officer for a further three years.

The bombs Major Knight had to deal with were often damaged and badly corroded. This meant the fuses were highly unstable, the balance-staffs might break at the slightest movement or the mainsprings wind down in an instant, resulting in detonation. The fuses were filled with picric acid which crystallised with age, so any friction between the crystals and the bomb casing as the fuse was withdrawn would cause the fuse to ignite like a struck match, with devastating results.

Ten years of defusing German bombs took their toll on this quiet hero and even decades after leaving the army he could not bear to have a ticking clock beside his bed.

Chapter Seven

Evacuees

Under the government's evacuation scheme, there had been long-standing plans for the transfer of children away from the south coast should the threat of air raids materialise. Those to be evacuated included schoolchildren and their teachers, mothers with under-fives, pregnant women, and the sick and infirm. The evacuation of London and other industrial cities began as early as September 1939, while the south coast followed suit after Dunkirk, when the threat of invasion increased.

AN URGENT APPEAL

BOROUGH OF STAFFORD

Government Evacuation Scheme

1,800 school children will be evacuated to Stafford in the event of air raids.

The number of householders who have placed their name on the Roll of those ready to receive unaccompanied school children has been very disappointing.

Billeting Officers, Reception Officers and their helpers are at present visiting householders with a view to surveying the accommodation now available and I earnestly appeal to everyone who has accommodation available to indicate their willingness to receive unaccompanied school children. I am bound to remind you that in default of voluntary offers compulsory powers would have to be used.

If a visitor has not yet called and you have not completed the form asking to be placed on the Roll, please notify the Town Clerk, Borough Hall either verbally or in writing of your offer of accommodation.

H. JOYNES,
Mayor.

Mayor's Parlour,
Stafford.
17th April, 1940.

In 1940 there was an 'urgent appeal' for places for evacuees from Ramsgate.

Under the scheme Stafford was initially to receive 1,568 children, teachers and helpers from Ramsgate, out of 3,500 evacuees from all areas bound for the county as a whole. However, according to figures produced by the county's director of education, by 18 September 1940 some 2,262 children had been evacuated from Ramsgate, 2,085 of whom had been billeted in Stafford.

The port of Ramsgate lay only 28 miles off enemy-occupied France and was bombed and later shelled on an almost daily basis. The town's chalk caves were turned into air raid shelters and were in regular use for almost the entire war. Meanwhile, the port's sandy beaches, once an adventure playground for children, were mined and fortified with barbed-wire entanglements against a possible invasion.

On the morning of Sunday, 2 June 1940 the children of Ramsgate attended farewell services with their parents before making their way to the railway station. The need for secrecy meant that the move was made at only two days' notice, and the children themselves knew nothing about the journey until that morning. After a tiring three-hour journey the train pulled into Stafford station, where the children disembarked noisily and were lined up by their teachers. Few if any of them had ever heard of Stafford before, and all they knew was that they were in the 'countryside' and a long way from home.

The evacuees were dressed in their Sunday Best and each carried a small suitcase containing their worldly goods. Everyone had a gas mask, worn around the neck in a cardboard box, and the children all had a luggage label tied to their clothes in case they became lost. An impressive reception party of local dignitaries lined the station platform to greet them, including Stafford's Mayor, Councillor Horace Joynes, and representatives of the Education and Health Committees.

The teachers then led a lengthy crocodile of children the short distance to Tenterbanks Girls' School. Here they were given a quick medical, which included the scrutiny of the inevitable nit nurse, before moving on to the old Meat Market where they were to receive light refreshments. Food shortages and the lack of advance warning meant that many could only be given milk and biscuits, which were wolfed down hungrily. By this time the excitement of the journey had worn off for many of the children, and the younger ones wept desperately for their mothers.

Then came the selection process. Lined up in ranks in the market, the children stood quietly while prospective foster parents walked along and made their choices. The wait to be chosen was upsetting and humiliating, and the desolation many felt at the time was to remain with some of them for the rest of their lives. Once allocated their places, the children were ferried by a fleet of buses, taxis and private cars to their temporary homes.

Stafford's schools were already crowded. On Monday, 3 June the Ramsgate staff met their new head teachers and delivered their pupil lists. The lack of additional classroom space meant that some lessons were initially conducted in school halls, chapels and even corridors. For many the summer of 1940 was one of extra gym, swimming lessons and nature walks.

St George's School, Ramsgate, transferred en masse to the old school rooms at St Mary's. Their teachers were supplemented by ladies who joined the previously all-male staff, while older teachers were recalled from retirement as the younger men enlisted into the Services. The five classrooms each had an open fire behind the teacher's desk, the pupils having to wear their overcoats, hats and mittens indoors during the winter to keep warm. Science classes were held in the new Technical College, while woodwork was taught in a building close to the railway station. Basic physical training exercises could be performed in the school courtyard, but football and cricket were played on the English Electric Sport and Welfare Club pitches. This involved a long walk down Lichfield Road to the southern outskirts of the town.

Clarendon House Girls' School also transferred its pupils and teachers to Stafford, occupying both the Oval and Baswich House on a time-share basis with the pupils of the Stafford Girls' High School, only returning to Ramsgate in January 1945. Meanwhile, Chatham House Boys' School similarly shared the King Edward VI Grammar School. At Tenterbanks School primary school pupils from Stafford occupied the ground floor, while older children from Ramsgate studied upstairs.

Every month the evacuee children wrote a letter home. Their teacher would write the school address on the blackboard, followed by 'Dear Mum and Dad, I hope you are well . . .'. After this rather formulaic start, the children could say whatever they wanted, describing their adventures or telling their parents what they thought of their new surroundings.

The sudden arrival of so many school-age children into the town inevitably caused logistical problems with organising lessons, but at least there were billeting allowances to help with the costs. These modest funds were intended to cover 'full board, lodgings and all necessary care and attention, including laundry and medical needs'. The provision of clothing and footwear, however, remained the responsibility of the children's parents. The local Women's Voluntary

Service (WVS), based on Greengate Street, had a small supply of clothes that could be used in emergencies.

The local newspaper ran a weekly half-page of Ramsgate news, helping to draw the two distant communities together. Fundraising events also linked the towns, with money raised in Stafford going to help stricken families in the coastal town and to the Ramsgate lifeboat appeal.

With the Battle of Britain won and the imminent threat of invasion fast receding, some of the Ramsgate evacuees returned to their homes by early 1941, with more going home by the end of the following year. Most, however, remained in Stafford until after D-Day, and some even made the town their permanent home.

Those who spent at least part of the war in Stafford remembered the Saturday morning matinees at the Odeon, swimming at the Royal Brine Baths, and playing in Victoria Park or in the woodlands around the town's ancient fortress. There was also the annual Bagnall's party to which the evacuees were invited, each receiving a gift presented by the Mayor.

The last wave of evacuees came to Stafford from London and the towns and cities that lay along 'Doodlebug alley', the area most prone to attack by Adolf Hitler's V1 revenge weapon. Around 325 evacuees arrived at Common station in mid-August 1944. Soon the Allies would overrun the V1 and V2 sites, heralding the slow trickle of returning evacuees, which would soon become a flood, as peace was restored.

Chapter Eight

Dunkirk

Throughout the period known as the Phoney War the British Expeditionary Force (BEF) was waiting in France, unable to go on the offensive because the government did not want to compromise Belgian neutrality. Meanwhile, the Germans were regrouping just over the border, awaiting the order for an all-out assault, which began on 10 May 1940 when 135 divisions crossed the Dutch and Belgian frontiers. The Luftwaffe targeted the Allied air forces on the ground, preventing them from flying reconnaissance missions and giving vital air support. Some of Stafford's first combat losses came at this time with the deaths of Pilot Officers John Boon and Frederick Ridley, both of whom died in daring daylight bombing raids just four days after Hitler had launched his Blitzkrieg.

In its retreat the Belgian army failed to destroy the vital bridges over the Albert Canal, thus allowing the German Panzer divisions to pour over them. The RAF flew suicidal missions in an attempt to blow the bridges, and whole squadrons were virtually wiped out in a desperate attempt to halt the German advance.

Pilot Officer Boon served with 105 Squadron. At 07.50 hours on 14 May he took off in one of four unescorted Fairey Battles with orders to bomb the vital bridges around Douzy. These aircraft carried a crew of three but were slow and vulnerable. This time luck was with them and all four reached their target unhindered, the German anti-aircraft gunners unable to find them in the morning fog. All the aircraft returned safely.

A second raid was mounted at 15.30 hours, this time including Fairey Battles from Frederick Ridley's 150 Squadron. They were joined by eight Blenheims and by a number of Hawker Hurricanes of 1 and 73 Squadrons. By now the bridges were being protected by Messerschmitt Bf 109s of I and III/JG53. During the ensuing combat, pilots from I Gruppe claimed seven Fairey Battles destroyed, with the two Staffordians among their victims. These men died trying to stem the tide of the German advance but it was unstoppable, overwhelming Belgium and France within a matter of days.

Meanwhile, the men of the BEF were fighting bravely in defence of

Dunkirk

French soil. During one counter-attack Captain Colin Birch of Stafford and another soldier of the 2nd Battalion, North Staffordshire Regiment, were wounded. Both men lay in open ground under heavy fire until gallantly rescued by Corporal J. Wade of the same regiment. Corporal Wade was later awarded the Distinguished Conduct Medal (DCM), the announcement being made in the local press.

As the heavily outnumbered men of the BEF were pushed back towards Dunkirk, and their ammunition started to run low, the Germans threatened to overrun and capture an entire army. With the fate of two local battalions hanging in the balance, the pages of the *Stafford Advertiser* and *Chronicle* were read with mounting anxiety. On 9 June the first comprehensive lists of evacuated personnel reached Stafford, bringing relief for many. Others were not so lucky.

Staffordians Thomas James Manktelow of the 1st Battalion, Royal East Lancashire Regiment, and William Robinson of the Royal Engineers were among those lost during the rearguard actions designed to protect the troops making their way towards the beaches.

Among those who fought bravely during the Dunkirk evacuation was John Downing, whose elder brother George had served in the Stafford Battery of the Royal Artillery during the First World War. George had won the Military Medal for saving the life of Lord Harrowby; John would go one better and win the Distinguished Conduct Medal.

As a teenager John decided to follow in his brother's footsteps, becoming first a member of the Stafford Battery and later joining the Regulars. He made steady progress through the ranks, to become a sergeant and later a battery quartermaster-sergeant. He saw service in Malaya, Singapore and Malta, as well as spending time on Home Defence. His unit set sail for France with the BEF on 13 September 1939 and John himself was one of the very first British 'Tommies' to land in France; little did he then know that he would be among the last to leave.

Battery Quartermaster Sergeant John Downing won his DCM defending the Dunkirk Mole with his anti-aircraft gun, allowing thousands of men to escape. (Reproduced by courtesy of Anne Kennington)

Serving with an anti-aircraft gun, John was in the thick of the action in the historic defence of the Mole in Dunkirk harbour. It was from here that thousands of men were able to board small craft to carry them out to the deep-draught Royal Navy vessels that were unable to embark troops from the shallows. Throughout the evacuation German long-range guns pounded the town and beaches of

Dunkirk, paying particular attention to the Mole, while the Luftwaffe relentlessly dive-bombed the troops, Royal Navy ships and the beaches. Time and time again Junkers Ju 87 Stuka dive-bombers tried to put the Mole out of action, and it was largely through BQMS Downing's gritty determination that it remained in use as a means of escape. Refusing to give in, John kept his gun firing throughout the long air raids, either putting the Stuka pilots off their aim or forcing them to pick less well defended targets. The bombardment intensified during 1 and 2 June but John and his battery refused to be silenced, fighting off the bombers until all their ammunition was expended and they were given orders to evacuate. This John did, but not before 'spiking' his gun.

John's exploits lifted the spirits of the men on the Mole, the relentless firing of his battery becoming symbolic of the determination of the men of the BEF to escape to fight another day. During debriefing, a number of officers cited John's gallantry, recommending him for the award of the Distinguished Conduct Medal, which is second only to the Victoria Cross. This award was later promulgated in the Supplement to the *London Gazette* dated 11 July 1940. The recommendation for John's DCM read:

> Sergeant Downing displayed great gallantry in maintaining the service of a gun of which he was Number 1, during the 1st and 2nd June 1940 at Dunkirk dockyard, whilst under heavy shell fire and low-flying bombing attacks of the enemy. He put up a very effective fire which dispersed several low-flying attacks on the Mole and undoubtedly saved it from severe damage.

News of the award only reached the county town via the press: John himself was a modest man, and hadn't even told his parents about the medal.

Not long after his return to England on one of the many 'little ships', John Downing received an invitation to attend an investiture at Buckingham Palace, where King George VI pinned the DCM on the chest of this quiet hero. He was to be summoned to London again later in the war, attending a number of prestigious events. He wrote about his experiences in a letter to his mother at 11 Browning Street:

> I have been having a marvellous time. I was among the 1,500 members of the whole ack ack [anti-aircraft] in the British Isles who were selected to attend the Lord Mayor of London's party a couple of weeks ago.
>
> Last Sunday I was also selected to be in charge of 47 picked men from the batteries in the brigade in the Battle of Britain parade. It was a very proud moment for me to march through the streets of London at the head of my men past the King and Queen. It was one of the proudest moments of my life.

Dunkirk

John Downing later served in the British Army of Occupation of the Rhine and retired from the Army in 1956, having completed no less than 25 years' unblemished service. In addition to his DCM, he was also awarded a Long Service Good Conduct Medal (LSGC) and the Meritorious Service Medal (MSM), and received a Commander-in-Chief's Commendation.

One of the men who escaped from the Mole was Private John Bambury of the 9th Surrey and Sussex Yeomanry. Pushed back by the German advance, his regiment had suffered a number of casualties and lost most of their guns to enemy action. Private Bambury later recalled:

> The last of our guns was knocked out by German tanks some miles from Dunkirk and the remaining members of the regiment were then told to make their own way to Dunkirk.
>
> Arriving on the beach our eyes were greeted by long lines of battle-weary troops slowly, oh so slowly wending their way towards the Mole, which was a concrete structure like a pier going into the sea.

Dodging from one fox-hole to another, Private Bambury finally reached the front of the queue at the shore end of the Mole. Here a naval officer was calmly sending thirty men at a time on to the remnants of the shattered structure, giving them strict instructions to move as quickly as possible down the walkway to where the boats lay in deeper water. Above them flew Stuka dive-bombers. Their only protection came from John Downing's anti-aircraft gun. Bambury recalled:

> As we reached about half-way we were shelled, and I found myself in the sea. Being a reasonably good swimmer I headed out to sea where more ships were waiting.
>
> On my way I saw two men making slow hard work of it and little progress, and realised then that one of them was just about all in. His mate was in little better condition. I swam over and between us we managed to reach a ship with a rope ladder hanging down its side. With a great deal of pushing and shoving we managed to get the third man out of the water and on to the ladder.
>
> At this moment I was picked up by a naval cutter and was conveyed to HMS *Vanquisher*, which was a destroyer. Here I was given my first satisfying meal for days. It consisted of a thick bully beef sandwich, and a mug of scalding hot tea.

John Bambury was one of the lucky ones. Some 30,000 men were lost during the evacuation, many of them killed on the beaches, others drowned when their would-be rescuers were sunk in mid-Channel.

Chapter Nine

The Battle of France and the Battle of Britain

Initial air support for the BEF had been provided by ten Fairey Battle light bomber squadrons of the Advance Air Strike Force (AASF). Later this contingent was changed to eight light bomber squadrons supported by 1 and 73 Squadrons flying Hawker Hurricanes. In addition there were four other Hurricane squadrons (85, 87, 607 and 615 Squadrons), along with four Bristol Blenheim squadrons. Together they made up the Air Component, which was directly under the British Commander-in-Chief, Viscount Gort VC. These squadrons were further supported by 2 Group's bombers, based in England.

While there were occasional reconnaissance and other missions across the frontiers, the RAF aircraft were largely confined to French airspace, flying regular sorties from a string of airfields behind the Maginot Line, a wall of supposedly impregnable military defences along the border with Germany. The first flights over the German border led to heavy casualties among the RAF's light bomber squadrons.

David Blomeley

Fighter pilot David Blomeley fought in both the Battle of France and the later Battle of Britain. As a boy, David attended King Edward VI's Grammar School before working briefly for South and Stubbs, Agricultural Valuers and Surveyors. When he was old enough to enlist, Blomeley joined the RAF on a short-service commission.

At the end of his training Blomeley was posted to 1 Squadron at Tangmere. Seven days after Britain's entry into the war, his squadron took its Hawker Hurricanes over to France as part of the AASF, flying regular patrols along the Franco-Belgian border. On 8 April 1940, following brief postings to 92 and 25 Squadrons, David joined 151 Squadron at North Weald, still flying Hawker Hurricanes.

David's new Commanding Officer was Squadron Leader Edward 'Teddy' Donaldson, a pre-war RAF Display Team leader and back-to-back winner of the Brooke-Popham Air-to-Air Gunnery trophy.

The Battle of France and the Battle of Britain

Conscious of the impending war with Germany, Teddy put his squadron through an intensive programme of training, including mock combats and gunnery practice.

David Blomeley was one of eleven pilots seconded to 607 Squadron following that unit's decimation during the first phase of the Battle of France. He flew to Vitry aerodrome in France in the company of Flying Officer K.E. Newton and Pilot Officer R.N.H. 'Buck' Courtney of 151 Squadron. They arrived in the early hours of 14 May and were quickly back in the air as at 09.00 hours fifteen Herschel Hs 123s of II (S)/LG2 approached Louvain at low level, with a formation of Heinkel He IIIs of I and III/KG27 flying some way above them. Some forty-five Messerschmitt Bf 109s were also on the scene. All available pilots were scrambled and engaged the enemy, with ten German aircraft being claimed as damaged or destroyed. A contemporary newspaper recorded the events from Pilot Officer Courtney's perspective: 'When he returned after the successful flight, he found that his base had been bombed and the Hurricane he had flown a short time previously – in which were his spare clothes and personal belongings – had been wrecked by bombs.' But there was no respite. At 15.35 hours 607 Squadron joined 3 and 87 Squadrons in providing a fighter escort to a formation of twenty-nine Battles from 218, 103 and 88 Squadrons on bombing raids.

On the following day Blomeley's squadron escorted a Blenheim photo-reconnaissance sortie to Wavre and Louvain. It was a dangerous mission, as such flights were made at tree-top level. The squadron's CO, Squadron Leader L.E. Smith, was shot down and killed while in combat with a Messerschmitt Bf 109 of III/JG 53 near Dinant. The remainder of the day was spent in trying to protect the BEF and French 1st Army along the Gembloux–Wavre–Louvain line, with a number of patrols taking place, at least one of which, at 16.30 hours, led to an engagement with the enemy.

On 16 May a number of patrols were flown from Vitry, while in the afternoon five Dornier Do 17s were engaged at around 14.30 hours, another formation of Dornier Do 17s being attacked by three 607 Squadron Hurricanes at 17.00 hours. The

Pilot Officer David Blomeley was seconded to 607 Squadron during the Battle of France, later returning to 151 Squadron. He claimed fifteen enemy aircraft damaged or destroyed by December 1943.

The Hawker Hurricane flown by David Blomeley. (Reproduced by courtesy of Anne Kennington)

air campaign remained intense, with each pilot flying at least two or three operational sorties every day, while the lack of spare parts meant that Hurricanes had to be taken up even if they were in a damaged state of repair.

Having already flown an escort mission at 04.25 hours on 17 May, the Hurricanes of 607 Squadron were in the air once more at 09.30 hours when Dornier Do 17s were sighted to the north-east of Cambrai. These dealt with, a number of low-level reconnaissance sorties were flown for the army. At 14.30 hours the squadron was once more in combat, this time against a formation of Heinkel He IIIs.

Further patrols were flown on 18 May, with Vitry airfield now being used by a combined force of 56/229 and 111/253 Squadrons. At 15.00 hours 151 Squadron also arrived, although there was little time for David to become reacquainted with his pals as the aerodrome was attacked by Dornier Do 17s.

The day had been a hectic one for the pilots of 607 Squadron, who suffered further attacks while trying to gain enough height to defend Vitry airfield. There were a number of other combats, including those with Dornier Do 17s of III/KG76 at 07.40 hours and again at 10.15 hours, while Messerschmitt Bf 110s and Bf 109s were engaged at 16.30

hours. That evening, battle-weary and with few serviceable aircraft left, the squadron moved to Norrent-Fontes.

Flying with a composite unit from 56/229 Squadrons, 607 Squadron's new CO, Squadron Leader Fidler, led A Flight in an engagement with Messerschmitt Bf 109s of I (J) LG2 during which two enemy aircraft were destroyed for the loss of one Hurricane. Squadron Leader Fidler himself was shot down and taken prisoner west of Tournai; it was the squadron's second such loss in a matter of four days. At 16.20 hours B Flight successfully jumped a formation of Junkers Ju 88s of III/LG1, destroying several aircraft.

Operating from Norrent-Fontes on 20 May, Blomeley flew alongside pilots of 615 Squadron, led by Squadron Leader Kayll, attacking the German troops advancing along the Cambrai–Arras road. That evening, following more patrols, the squadron received orders to evacuate. Flying Officer Newton and Pilot Officers Courtney and Blomeley were ordered to fly to Croydon and then to report to North Weald. Courtney later recalled that 'the four Hurricanes we flew back were immediately scrapped as they counted 87 bullet holes in one of them, which only had three engine bearings left'.

During its time in France the squadron had destroyed forty-one enemy aircraft with a further sixteen unconfirmed. Seventeen Hurricanes had been lost, with five brave pilots dead and another three captured. In one hectic week David Blomeley had completed 31 hours

The medals won by David Blomeley included the Distinguished Flying Cross and the Air Force Cross.

The pilots of 151 Squadron pictured in June 1940. Third from the left is the squadron's commanding officer, Squadron Leader 'Teddy' Donaldson, and third from the right is David Blomeley.

of operational flying and claimed five enemy aircraft damaged or destroyed.

Back with 151 Squadron at North Weald, Blomeley flew to Boulogne as a Blenheim escort on 29 May, destroying a Messerschmitt Bf 110 over Dunkirk. Five days later the squadron flew a similar mission to Rouen, during which Blomeley destroyed a Messerschmitt Bf 109.

However, his run of good luck couldn't last for ever and on 8 June, while escorting Bristol Blenheims on a bombing raid to Amiens, Blomeley's Hurricane (P3315) was hit by anti-aircraft fire. He lost altitude and became separated from the rest of his squadron before being hit by French gunners; his log-book indicates that he was also attacked by a Messerschmitt Bf 109. Baling out some 15 miles south-west of Amiens, Blomeley found himself under fire from French soldiers. His parachute caught fire and he landed awkwardly, injuring his ankle. The French rifle-fire intensified when Blomeley hit the ground, but eventually he made his voice heard. Finally given shelter by the French, he tried to get some sleep. He was woken later that evening by the sound

The Battle of France and the Battle of Britain

of voices speaking in German, and discovered the French had fled and left him behind.

Undaunted, Blomeley climbed through a window and headed for a cropped field. Moving by night in the shelter of hedgerows and ditches, he made his way towards the coast, eventually linking up with the remnants of the 51st Highland Division and escaping via Cherbourg. By 20 June he was back flying with 151 Squadron.

On 28 June he patrolled Calais escorting a formation of Blenheims, and two days later was over Amiens, protecting another Blenheim raid. On 9 July 151 Squadron flew on a convoy escort patrol, and Blomeley recorded in his log-book that he had a hand in the destruction of two Messerschmitt Bf 109s. Another convoy patrol was flown on the following day, with Blomeley claiming a Messerschmitt Bf 110 as 'smoking'. During another patrol on 12 July he claimed a Messerschmitt Bf 109 destroyed, while on the following day he engaged and hit a Messerschmitt Bf 109, a Messerschmitt Bf 110 and a Heinkel He 111. Two days later a patrol led to the destruction of a Heinkel He 111 and a Dornier Do 17. It didn't all go his way, though, and during a dogfight on 25 July Blomeley's Hurricane was damaged by return fire and he had to break off the engagement and make for North Weald, where he landed safely.

Patrolling on 3 August Blomeley claimed another Messerschmitt Bf 109 destroyed, and two days later he wrote the words 'hood shot off' against an entry in his log-book. Despite this near-miss, he flew a second patrol later that day, noting a Messerschmitt Bf 109 and a Messerschmitt Bf 110 damaged or destroyed.

David Blomeley's last combat sortie with 151 Squadron came on 16 August, when his Hurricane was shot down but he managed to bale out. Following a brief spell in hospital, and with his tour of operations completed, Blomeley was posted to 9 FTS Hullavington as an instructor. During the Battle of Britain Blomeley had added five 'kills' to his growing total, having shot at or damaged many more enemy aircraft.

Subsequently Blomeley retrained as a night-fighter pilot and converted on to twin-engine aircraft. He was posted to 604 Squadron, flying Mosquito twin-engine night-fighters, and took part in intruder raids deep into enemy-occupied Europe. He teamed up with Flying Officer Birrell and together they destroyed four enemy aircraft during 1943.

David Blomeley was awarded the Distinguished Flying Cross in October 1943, with the *Stafford Chronicle* reporting that, 'Of the thirteen aircraft definitely confirmed as having been shot down, his last

47

No. 151 Squadron taking off on a scramble from North Weald, 1940.

Nos 56 and 151 Squadrons at North Weald during July 1940.

No. 151 Squadron pilots awaiting the scramble, July 1940.

two were sent down into the North Sea within a period of ten minutes.' Blomeley's de Havilland Mosquito now sported fifteen swastikas and the inevitable nose artwork depicting Popeye swinging his fist accompanied by the word 'Blom'.

'Gil' Gilbert

Ernest 'Gil' Gilbert also flew combat sorties during both the Battle of France and the later Battle of Britain. Gil was one of the so-called 'Halton Brats', who made their way up through the ranks to become sergeant-pilots. Having enlisted as an apprentice aircraft fitter in the RAF on 1 September 1928, Gil was selected to retrain as a pilot and was posted to 5 Pilot Training School (PTS) at RAF Sealand in October 1934. He proved to be a 'natural' pilot, his log-book recording that he made his first solo flight after only 9½ hours' flying time.

Gil was awarded his pilot's brevet on 22 August 1935, having then completed nearly 89 hours' solo flying. His first posting as a sergeant pilot came when he joined 6 Squadron in Ismalia. When 64 Squadron was reformed at Heliopolis in March 1936, it was composed of Gil's flight along with another flight from 29 Squadron. Gil returned to the UK in September 1936, his new unit being based at Martlesham Heath as part of the Home Defence force.

Gil was still flying Bristol Blenheims when war was declared and it wasn't until late March 1940 that his unit finally received its first

Supermarine Spitfires. There then followed a period of retraining while the pilots worked on methods of attack and formation flying, as well as getting in some much-needed gunnery practice and honing their skills in air-to-air combat. Gil flew his first Spitfire patrol on 30 March 1940, his first combat coming only a few weeks later. As a flight sergeant, Gil sometimes led the squadron into combat. His log-book reveals that 64 Squadron played a major part in the events of the summer of 1940, when the future of Britain teetered on a knife-edge:

21/5/40	Two Ju 88s sighted but [they] escaped into cloud. Calais-Bologne. Chased another. Two deflection shots.
30/5/40	Dunkirk-Furness 9 aircraft with self leading.
30/5/40	Gravesend 64 and 610 Squadron on patrol over Dunkirk.
31/5/40	Dunkirk-Furness. Same formation. No enemy aircraft but accurate anti-aircraft fire.
12/6/40	Various Heinkel intercepted. ½ kill to Me ½ to Laws. [Sergeant Andrew Laws was a sergeant pilot with 64 Squadron. He later won the Distinguished Flying Medal and was commissioned. He was killed in action later in the war.]
17/7/40	Local flying over Brighton. F.O. Taylor shot down and wounded.
5/8/40	Self leading Squadron.
7/8/40	Self leading Squadron on aerodrome defence. 6 Spitfires attacked 5 Hurricanes (mock dog-fighting). Excellent dog-fight. Hurricanes too easy.
15/8/40	Mid-Channel Squadron attacked 100 Me 109s. I saw Me 109 shooting at a Spitfire. Shot him down but Me 109 behind me fired at me. One bullet removed coolant gauge from dashboard and cockpit filled with steam. Lost height towards Dover where he departed. Stood up in cockpit to land aircraft at Hawkinge with no air speed indicator. A most unpleasant experience. [Gil discovered later that a shell splinter had damaged his parachute; had he elected to jump to 'safety', it would have shredded on opening and he would almost certainly have fallen to his death.]
16/8/40	Chased 2 Hurricanes. 'A' Flight got 5 Me 109s.
16/8/40	Attacked approximately 100 Heinkel IIIs. Did No. 4 attack with Sergeant Whelan – damaged rear section of Heinkel. No observed result. Formation apparently escorted by Me 110s – never saw them nor them us.
18/8/40	Kenley bombed. Attacked rear section of 3 Heinkels – port starboard engine of number 2 out of action. Attacked him

Ernest 'Gil' Gilbert responding to a scramble. His unit was equipped with Bristol Blenheims until as late as March 1940, and the pilots had little time to adjust to their new single-seater fighters before being thrust into the Battle of France.

Gil Gilbert in dispersals, waiting for the next scramble.

as he broke formation. He dived straight in from 6,000 feet. Missed church just south of Biggin Hill by 20 yards.

18/8/40   Returned to Kenley – 49 unexploded bombs on aerodrome. Dornier 17 crashed just behind dispersals.

27/10/40   After Dornier 17. Limpenny shot him down.

11/11/40   Attacked 30 + Ju 87s. No casualties.

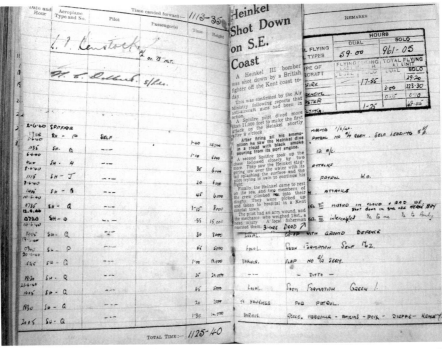

Pilot's log-book belonging to Gil Gilbert. The entries for 10 and 12 July record interceptions of two Heinkel 111s; on the latter date Gilbert and Andy Laws were credited with a 'shared' aircraft destroyed.

The destruction of a Heinkel He 111 by Sergeant Andy Laws and Gil Gilbert was recorded in one of the local newspapers, and Gil proudly pasted the cutting into his log-book:

Heinkel shot down on SE Coast

A Heinkel 111 bomber was shot down by a British fighter off the Kent coast today. This was confirmed by the Air Ministry following reports that anti-aircraft guns had been in action.

A Spitfire pilot dived more than 11,000 feet to make the first attack on the Heinkel shortly after 8 o'clock.

After firing all his ammunition he saw the Heinkel dive into cloud with black smoke pouring from its port engine.

A second Spitfire took up the chase followed closely by two more. They saw the Heinkel staggering slowly low over the water with its tail splashing the surface and the pilot trying in vain to continue his flight.

Finally the Heinkel came to rest on the sea and two members of the crew climbed out on to their dinghy. They were picked up and taken to hospital in a Kent coastal town.

The pilot had an arm wound and the mechanic, who weighed 18 st., a head injury. A local fisherman rescued them.

The press cutting was annotated by Gil with the words '3 more dead'.

Gil's flying skills and devotion to duty were acknowledged by a promotion-in-the-field to the rank of pilot officer with effect from 26 August 1940, just after he had shot down his second confirmed Heinkel He 111.

With his tour of operations completed, Gil was selected for a pilot instructors' course at the Central Flying School (CFS), Upavon, taking up his appointment there on 1 December 1940. Fortunately, his temperament was ideally suited to this role and he was to fly as an instructor from January 1941 until September 1944, spending part of this time with 21 (P) AFU at Wheaton Aston.

George Hassall Nelson-Edwards

George Hassall Nelson-Edwards was born in Stafford on 8 March 1918 and was educated at Shrewsbury School and Brasenose College, Oxford, where he learned to fly in the University Air Squadron. He was called-up into full-time service on the outbreak of the war in September 1939. He was posted to 79 Squadron on 1 August 1940 and his first combat victory came on 28 August when he destroyed a Herschel Hs 59.

On 31 August Nelson-Edwards was in combat over Biggin Hill when his Hurricane (N2345) was shot down. He was slightly injured. In combat again on 27 September his aircraft was hit by return fire from a Heinkel He 111. He was rescued from the Irish Sea off Milford Haven by the crew of the SS *Dartford*.

Promoted to the rank of flight lieutenant on 26 September 1941, Nelson-Edwards was given command of 93 Squadron on 1 June the following year. His unit took part in the invasion of North Africa as part of the Anglo-American assault force that landed in Algiers on 13 November 1943. Here he claimed a Junkers Ju 88 destroyed on 26 November, with a second confirmed on 4 December.

On 26 February 1943 he was awarded the Distinguished Flying Cross and returned to England, where he became the RAF's Liaison Officer working alongside the 9th Air Force, North-West Europe. Nelson-Edwards retired as a wing commander in 1960.

Chapter Ten

No. 395 (Stafford) Squadron, ATC

If the RAF were to survive what was already being predicted to be a three-year war, it needed a training-ground for Britain's youth. The Stafford Air Training Corps (ATC) was formed on 4 February 1941 as part of the government's call to foster such groups in the community. The guest of honour at the first meeting, held in the Lecture Hall of Stafford Library, was Battle of Britain fighter ace Squadron Leader Edward 'Teddy' Donaldson DSO. At the end of the lecture Mr H. Blomeley, headmaster of the Corporation Street School, was able to speak to 'Teddy' Donaldson, his son's CO at 151 Squadron during the Battle of France and later Battle of Britain.

Officers of Stafford ATC. Left to right: Flight Lieutenant Richard Ingar, Flight Lieutenant H. Lorton and Flying Officer H.C. Thomas.

Mr Richard Ingar, one of the wartime officers with the Stafford Squadron, recalled:

The idea was to form a voluntary youth organisation for youngsters interested in aviation to help provide practical training which would be of use both in civilian and service life, encouraging their spirit of adventure and at the same time developing qualities of leadership and teamwork.

No. 395 (Stafford) Squadron, ATC

Soon 395 Squadron, ATC had a nucleus of half a dozen officers and some 100–150 recruits. The officers included former First World War pilots John M. Brown, H. Lorton and Scott Gough, all of whom had flown in action at a time when the life expectancy of a combat pilot was measured in hours rather than days or weeks. These men were all seasoned pilots and were greatly respected by their fellow officers and the cadets alike.

The squadron met every Monday and Thursday between 19.00 hours and 21.00 hours at King Edward VI's Grammar School. Through Mr Blomeley's influence, it also used the Corporation Street School's playground for drill, while premises in Glover Street were utilised for some of its training exercises. Much of the training was carried out by the squadron's own officers, with the RAF providing additional supervision along with rifles, training equipment, funding and, most importantly, instruction manuals. With the aid of these manuals the ATC cadets learned about the principles of flight, meteorology, navigation, the mechanics of the aero-engine, radio operation, Morse Code, signalling with flags and, of course, flying. Occasional visits to RAF airfields provided the recruits with the opportunity to gain flying time as passengers or in gliders. Various proficiency badges were issued on the satisfactory completion of their courses and suitable cadets could also be promoted to NCOs. An appeal was launched on 9 May 1942 in order to raise the £75 needed to purchase a glider, which would give the boys air experience prior to their possible selection for air crew duties once they had enlisted in the RAF.

Some of the former members of the Stafford Squadron included Eric Johnson BEM, DFC, AFC, Joe Willshaw DFC and Trevor Myatt DFM. Another airman whose flying career began with 395 Squadron, ATC was Sergeant Roy Hill, who was later lost on the Nuremburg raid.

In mid-1941 the squadron received an influx of fifty recruits, who came to the town with the evacuees from Ramsgate, bringing with them one of their own officers, Flying Officer Faulkner. A year later girls between the ages of 14 and 17 were able to prepare for service with the WAAF by joining the Women's Junior Air Corps, their inaugural meeting being held on 10 May 1942.

In the postwar years 395 Squadron found a permanent home at 16 MU, RAF Stafford, and became known as the 'Roy Hill' Squadron in memory of the young air gunner who lost his life over Germany.

Chapter Eleven

'The Staffordian'

It was at the height of the Battle of Britain that the people of the county town embarked on their first major fundraising project of the war. The *Stafford Chronicle* of 20 August 1940 carried the following announcement, made on behalf of the Mayor, Councillor Horace Joynes:

> I propose a meeting of interested people on Monday next, 26 August, at 8pm in the Committee Rooms of the Borough Hall, with a view to officially launching this appeal.
>
> As everyone is aware, £5,000 is required to purchase one of these machines and I am confident that the amount will be very quickly raised in this district.
>
> It appears to me that there is a general desire amongst the people of Stafford and District that we should purchase a Spitfire aeroplane, and present this to the Nation. Consequently I have agreed to launch an appeal for this purpose. I am sure that all will agree that this is a laudable objective. Words are not enough to show our appreciation of what the RAF are doing for us, but with the purchase of another aeroplane we are not only showing our appreciation, but we are giving them practical help.

As Mayor of Stafford, Councillor Horace Joynes headed the council during the first eighteen months of the war.

Perhaps the choice of venue was a little intimidating for ordinary townsfolk, as the meeting was later reported to have been 'very poorly attended'. By 27 August only £389 4s 10¹/₄d had been raised. A renewed appeal and a series of dances and other events had brought in £1,310 17s 9d by 5 September, while nine days later on 14 September Stafford held a Flag Day, while a Whist Drive took place on the 18th.

The coffers received a further boost when the remains of a downed German bomber were displayed in St John's Market on Saturday, 21 September and on the following Tuesday; admission to view the remains cost a shilling for adults and 3d for the under-15s. On 28 September 1940 the *Stafford Chronicle* reported:

'The Staffordian'

Bomber Helps Fighters

The wrecked German bomber which sprawled its carcass in the Market Hall to such grand effort is having a truly beneficial effect on the Stafford and District Spitfire Fund. During the weekend alone it was the means of raising £205, contributed by somewhere about 5,000 people, and the people responsible for gathering the skeleton are quite hopeful that that sum will have been doubled by the time the German bomber is shovelled on to its travelling carriage and transported elsewhere to carry on its good work for the British RAF. The fund at the time of writing was on the sunny side of £3,000, and I should not be surprised if it does not reach £4,000 or so before another week is out. Just as the Spitfire is the speediest and most formidable fighter, so should the local fund be the

These press advertisements were produced as part of Stafford's campaign to raise funds for a Supermarine Spitfire.

speediest and most successful ever to have been inaugurated in the borough. As I said last week, 'Rally round and make your (financial) presence felt at the Ancient High House'.

With only £600 outstanding, a fundraising concert was held at the Odeon Theatre on Sunday, 6 October. At the end of the performance by the RAF Band, the Mayor of Stafford, Councillor Horace Joynes, announced that Mr J.F. Butler, the managing director of BRC, would contribute a further £10,000 if the town reached its target within the next fortnight.

Stafford duly dug deep and reached its target of £5,000 ahead of the deadline, thus guaranteeing that three Spitfires would be purchased for Fighter Command. The Mayor later announced that he had forwarded a cheque to Lord Beaverbrook, the Minister for Aircraft Production. The town could be very proud, as the whole project had taken less than two months to achieve. The Mayor publicly praised the people of the town for the 'splendid way they had supported the fund. All had rallied round magnificently, and the pennies of the children had helped as much as the pounds.'

Stafford's own Mark Vb Spitfire was given the name 'The

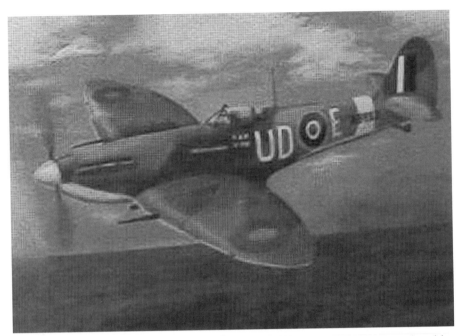

'The Staffordian' was paid for through the efforts of the townspeople. (Reproduced by courtesy of Anne Kennington)

Staffordian', which was duly painted on the side of the cockpit. The aircraft was delivered to 452 (Australian) Squadron at RAF Kenley on 5 August 1941, and was soon flown in combat. By this time, with the Battle of Britain already won, Fighter Command was busy taking the air war to the enemy with its so-called 'Circus' operations. The idea was for a dozen medium bombers to act as 'bait', escorted at a distance by some eighteen squadrons, or around 220 Spitfires in all. The bombers would go in and stir up the enemy, and when the Luftwaffe aircraft appeared the Spitfires would engage them in numbers, thus reducing the enemy's effective fighter cover and making Allied bomber raids slightly easier. The sight of so many British fighters over enemy-occupied Europe also acted as a morale boost for resistance fighters and others.

'The Staffordian' was one of the aircraft flown by Flight Lieutenant Keith Truscott, who had already destroyed five enemy fighters. A former Melbourne football star, Truscott was awarded the Distinguished Flying Cross on 4 October and was to become one of the most highly publicised members of the RAAF.

On 12 October, while flying with Circus no. 107 to the dockyards at Boulogne, Truscott added another two Messerschmitt Bf 109s to his tally. Circus no. 108 was flown on the following day, and was to escort six Blenheims to Arques. German fighters engaged the Australians on the return journey, shooting down one Spitfire for the loss of seven of their own aircraft, two of which fell to Truscott.

'The Staffordian'

Keith Truscott's luck ran out over the Channel on 13 November, on the return journey from an escort mission to Lille. The mêlée which ensued is best described in his own words, which first appeared in the press soon after he was shot down:

> Numerous hostile machines were coming down on my section, so I pulled round hard and fired at a range of about 50 yards on the first one. I saw one shell hit the engine and another burst in the vicinity of the cockpit. The aircraft seemed to explode, and then went down vertically, leaving a trail of smoke.

Within minutes 452 Squadron was again attacked. Manoeuvring away from a Messerschmitt Bf 109 on his tail, Truscott gave his would-be assailant a three-second burst which sent it into the sea.

Suddenly 'The Staffordian' shuddered. Truscott looked to his right only to see tell-tale bursts along the starboard wing. With his wing fragmenting he lost control and the plane went into a dive. Frantically the young Australian pulled at the canopy and climbed out ready to jump. Next thing he knew he was free-falling. His right hand reached for the ripcord and the parachute deployed with a bang. Truscott was picked up by one of the RAF's rescue launches after having spent about half an hour in the water.

Sadly, Keith Truscott did not survive the war. Having been awarded a Bar to his DFC and completed a tour of operations, he was posted back to Australia and light flying duties. While 'attacking' a Catalina flying boat during a mock dog-fight Truscott apparently misjudged his altitude. His aircraft plunged into the water and he was drowned.

Flight Lieutenant Keith Truscott DFC flew 'The Staffordian'. (Reproduced by courtesy of Anne Kennington)

Chapter Twelve

Submariners' Tales

Malta

The siege of Malta began on 11 June 1940, the day after Mussolini joined the Axis powers taking Italy into the war. Up until the mid-1930s Valletta in Malta had been the headquarters of the Royal Navy's Mediterranean Fleet, but now it was decided, given the proximity of the newly mobilised Italian Navy, which rivalled the Royal Navy, that Malta could not be defended and therefore resources should not be wasted in the attempt. Alexandria was in the ascendancy.

Staffordian Frank Plant was serving on HMS Perseus *when she was lost in the Mediterranean, not long after being adopted by the people of Stafford following Warship Week in 1941.*

Only some 4,000 soldiers and a few obsolete Gloster Gladiators were stationed on the island, with about five weeks' worth of food. Nevertheless, Malta remained a strategic threat, since its anti-shipping squadrons and Royal Navy submarines posed a potential threat to supply lines and communications between Europe, Italy and North Africa. Its loss would be a major blow to the British war effort. The siege intensified between April and November 1941, by which time the Axis powers held airfields in Cyrenaica and Libya.

In Stafford, as a result of the town's fundraising efforts during Warship Week, 4–10 November 1941, HM Submarine *Perseus* was adopted by the people of the town. *Perseus* may seem an unusual choice, but a small number of locals were submariners, among them Signalman Eric Eaton of HM Submarine *Shark*, and Lieutenant James Poole DSC and Bar of HM Submarine *Urge*. Only one

Staffordian, Engine Room Artificer 4th Class Frank Douglas Plant, is known to have been serving on *Perseus* at the time she was adopted by the people of Stafford. At the outbreak of hostilities Plant worked as an apprentice at Dorman Diesel's Tixall Road factory. In 1940, however, he joined the Royal Navy and later volunteered for duty in submarines.

Perseus, captained by Lieutenant-Commander E.C.F. Nicolay DSO, formed part of the 1st Submarine Flotilla operating out of Alexandria under the command of Sir Sidney Raw. Laid down in 1928, the submarine was launched at Barrow-in-Furness on 22 May 1929. One of the first vessels of the Parthian class, *Perseus* was fitted with a 4-inch Mk IV gun and carried fourteen Mk VIII torpedoes. But she was designed for ocean waters and not the confines of the Mediterranean, where her larger silhouette made her vulnerable in the calm seas.

This plaque in St Mary's churchyard, Stafford, is dedicated to the crew of HM Submarine Perseus.

In the early summer of 1941 the island of Crete fell, the final evacuation lasting until 3 June. The Royal Navy's Mediterranean fleet was very badly hit during the battle and subsequent evacuation, three cruisers and six destroyers being lost and a further two battleships and the fleet's only aircraft carrier being so badly damaged they had to be withdrawn from active service. The pressure already on the RAF in North Africa meant that the Royal Navy's 1st Submarine Flotilla was the only force left that was able to launch any sort of offensive in the Aegean Sea. Its all-out assault was to prove effective but costly, claiming forty of the seventy Navy submarines lost in that theatre during the whole of the Second World War.

Axis shipping was forced to run the gauntlet of such submarines as *Torbay*, *Triumph* and *Truant*, as well as the less successful *Perseus*, which nevertheless sported two enemy merchantmen on its 'Jolly Roger'. In the course of the war *Perseus* sank a total of 5,950 tons of shipping, along with supplies of ammunition and fuel oil that were vital to the *Regia Marina* and to the German *Afrika Korps* in North Africa.

Perseus's last patrol ended in tragedy. On 6 December 1941 she was sunk with the loss of all but one of her complement of fifty-three crewmen off Kephalonia in western Greece. She met the same fate as half the submarine casualties suffered in the confined waters of the

Mediterranean, striking a mine while recharging her batteries on the surface under cover of night. Four men who were in the Petty Officers' Mess survived the impact and quickly made their way to the stern section, which they sealed off as the crippled hull sank in 170 feet of water. Of these four men only one, Leading Stoker Johnny Capes, lived to tell the tale.

Capes, who was not a regular member of the crew but was working his passage, put on one of the sets of DESA escape gear and flooded the after-space before opening the rear escape hatch. Successfully rising to the surface, Capes then swam to Kephalonia, 7 or 8 miles away, where he was aided by Greek partisans.

When his story reached the Admiralty, Capes was recommended for the award of the British Empire Medal (BEM). He remained with the Royal Navy after the end of the war, but was always dogged by the rumour that he had never actually been on *Perseus*. Only when the wreck of the submarine was discovered, and the escape hatch was found open, exactly as Capes had described, was he finally vindicated. The wreck remains in deep water, and is officially classed as a War Grave.

Following the untimely loss of the *Perseus*, just a few weeks after Warship week, and in consultation with the Admiralty, Stafford adopted HM Submarine *Seraph* in early April 1942. This submarine was commanded by Captain Bill Jewell, who had links with the county town. *Seraph* was to become famous for her role in a number of clandestine operations. These included Operation 'Mincemeat', which was immortalised in the film 'The Man Who Never Was'.

James Poole DSC and Bar

It was during this phase of the battle for the Mediterranean that a second Staffordian, James Malcolm Stuart Poole, was killed in action. A former King Edward VI Grammar School pupil, Poole was a key member of the crew of HM Submarine *Urge*.

HM Submarine Urge *(right) moored alongside* HMS Upholder *in Malta.*

The Mediterranean was a dangerous place for any submarine. The tideless clear blue waters were often as flat as a mill-pond, so that from the air the feathered wake of a periscope breaking the surface could be seen for miles. The Allied vessels defending the Mediterranean included the S-class submarines based at Gibraltar, the T-class submarines based at Alexandria, and the U-class submarines of the 10th Submarine Flotilla operating under Commander G.W.G. Simpson, CO of Malta Forces Submarine, and based at Lazaretto Creek, not far from Malta's Grand Harbour of Valletta.

HM Submarine *Urge*, commanded by Lieutenant Commander E.P. Tomkinson RN, DSO and Bar, was the second highest-scoring Allied submarine serving in the Mediterranean, behind the legendary HM Submarine *Upholder*, commanded by Lieutenant Commander Malcolm David Wanklyn VC, DSO and two Bars. *Urge*'s crucial tasks included running supplies and key personnel to the besieged island of Malta, and hunting down and destroying Axis shipping.

On 18 April 1941 *Urge* torpedoed and sank the 10,000-ton Italian tanker *Franco Martelli* off Brest, while on her way to join the main flotilla, *Unique*, *Utmost*, *Ursula* and *Upholder*, already on station. The latter was yet to sink an enemy vessel but would soon open her account. Lieutenant Commander Tomkinson's first patrol out of Malta took his submarine to the waters between Pantelleria and Lampedusa. Here he located several Italian cruisers with a screen of destroyers. The water was very calm and his periscope trail was observed by the convoy's air cover and so he was forced to crash-dive. Waiting for his opportunity to strike, Tomkinson gradually brought *Urge* back up to periscope depth, and quickly took a 360-degree view of the scene. What he saw was the biggest enemy convoy yet encountered by the flotilla: two medium transporters and two tankers with an escort of five destroyers.

A tanker and a transporter lay almost directly in his path. Taking a bearing on the enemy, Tomkinson ordered the periscope down as he calculated the best firing pattern to ensure maximum effect. He fired two pairs of torpedoes. Four successive explosions were heard and the two vessels burst into flames, both later sinking. The destroyers quickly went onto the offensive, firing a wide pattern of depth-charges as they hunted for the unseen submarine which had wrought so much havoc. The barrage was fierce but brief, with the escort breaking off the engagement to pick up survivors as *Urge* silently slipped away.

The search to re-establish contact with the convoy of destroyers and cruisers was rewarded on the following day when the enemy was once more located by *Urge*. It was a potent force and so Lieutenant

Commander Tomkinson emptied all four torpedo tubes in a broad fan and quickly took evasive action. The torpedoes ran straight and true. Unfortunately two missed completely, while the remaining two sank one of the escorting destroyers.

Meanwhile, *Utmost* had run into a newly laid minefield in shallow waters to the north of Sicily. When she finally returned to Malta, her captain, Lieutenant Commander R.D. Cayley, reported the minefield's location to Commander Simpson, who immediately banned the 10th Submarine Flotilla from these waters and ordered the crews of *Utmost*, *Upholder* and *Urge* to find a way through it at all costs. When Simpson asked who would take the lead, Cayley immediately jumped in ahead of Wanklyn and Tomkinson. The three submarines would set off at 24-hour intervals. Miraculously all three submarines found a safe channel through to the Tyrrhenian Sea.

On a later patrol during the summer of 1941 *Urge* attacked another convoy and was able to fire four torpedoes in rapid succession. Three struck their targets, but the fourth nearly destroyed *Urge* as it jammed in the firing tube with its engine running. With just seconds before it detonated, Tomkinson quickly gave the order to surface. Then Lieutenant Poole was able to guide the helmsman through a sufficiently violent manoeuvre to shake it free. *Urge* then crash-dived immediately in full view of the enemy, and somehow managed to avoid their depth-charges. During the same patrol *Urge* engaged and sank another large enemy transport vessel.

As she approached Malta at the end of this patrol, navigation was made easier by the glowing fires of the naval base at Valletta and at Lazaretto Creek, which acted as a beacon. The submarine entered the base flying her 'Jolly Roger', her recent combat victories proudly displayed.

Urge soon added a dagger to her 'Jolly Roger', to represent a covert operation. On the night of 26/27 July 1941 she took four Commandos and their kit to Taormina; when she surfaced, the four commandos took to canoes and made landfall north of the town. They hid their canoes and crept to their target, an important railway tunnel. Charges set, the four men made their escape. The explosives did their job and destroyed a train and the tunnel.

On 27 August *Urge* attacked the Italian tanker *Pozarica* with torpedoes, but without success. On the following day Tomkinson located the Italian passenger ship *Aquitania*, which was hit and damaged. A third attack was launched on 29 August when the Italian troop transporter *Victoria* was engaged off Capri island. However, on this occasion the torpedoes missed their target.

In recognition of his successes as second officer on HM Submarine *Urge*, Lieutenant James Malcolm Stuart Poole RN gained the Distinguished Service Cross, the award being promulgated in the *London Gazette* of 28 November 1941.

A later patrol saw *Urge* attack and damage the Italian merchant ship *Margola* off Kuriat. Lieutenant Poole was in action again on 14 December 1941, when *Urge* engaged the Italian battleship *Vittorio Veneto*; she fired a salvo of torpedoes, one of which struck and damaged its target.

In late December *Uphold* and *Urge* went out on exercises with HMS *Beryl*. These exercises concluded on 28 December 1941, and the two submarines were approaching Lazaretto Creek on the surface when a radio intercept was forwarded to them: a German reconnaissance aircraft had spotted them and a formation of Messerschmitt Bf 109s was ready to pounce. Tomkinson barked out the command and *Urge* crash-dived. Woodward, who was on watch, raced down the conning tower ladder, slamming the hatch down behind him. *Upholder* was less fortunate and was hit by several cannon shells; one exploded inside the submarine, wounding several crewmen.

Urge returned to Malta.

While the submarines were moored at Lazaretto Creek, the crews were billeted in nearby houses, with the officers in hotels. However, there was always a skeleton crew – one officer, one artificer and an able seaman – left on board in case of emergencies. The growing intensity of air raids on the docked submarines led to orders being issued on 6 March for them to be submerged in deep-water berths with half their crew aboard unless they were undergoing major repairs.

On 1 April 1942, while on patrol north of Sicily, the crew of HM Submarine *Urge* added to their growing tally by torpedoing the Italian light cruiser *Giovanni delle Bande Nere*. She sank off the Italian coast near Stromboli.

Intelligence sources informed Commander Simpson of a convoy leaving Tripoli and the submarines *Thrasher*, *Upholder* and *Urge* were ordered to intercept it. At about 06.00 hours on 14 April a shock-wave was felt through the hulls of *Thrasher* and *Urge* as a depth-charge exploded some distance away. A further explosion was heard about an hour later. The explosions were repeated every hour or so until a sustained attack began at about 16.00 hours, lasting for an hour or so.

On 18 April Italian radio stations broadcast the news that an Allied submarine had been sunk in the central Mediterranean. It later came to light that Lieutenant Commander Wanklyn's *Upholder* had been discovered and sunk by depth-charges from the Italian torpedo boat *Pegaso*. She was on her twenty-fifth patrol, having sent twenty-one enemy vessels (128,353 tons) to the bottom of the Mediterranean.

Unaware of the fate of Wanklyn and his crew, *Urge* continued her patrol and was involved in an attack on the tanker *San Giusto* in the eastern Mediterranean on 29 April. The engagement led to an unsuccessful attack by Italian bombers.

By late April it was decided that Lazaretto Creek was no longer serviceable as a submarine base due to the incessant air raids, and on 1 May *Urge*, *Una*, *P31*, *P34* and *P35* left the creek and headed for their new base at Alexandria. Sadly, *Urge* was never heard of again. During her twenty patrols she had destroyed two cruisers, a destroyer, a transport, five supply ships and two tankers: a total of 74,669 tons. No one knows the exact fate of Lieutenant Poole and his fellow officers and crew, but they are believed to have died on 6 May. It is possible that the submarine struck a mine while recharging her batteries on the surface at night. Another possibility is that she too fell victim to the *Pegaso* while in the eastern Mediterranean.

When she failed to arrive at Alexandria, HMS *Urge* was reported as 'overdue' but eventually her status was changed to 'lost'. In September 1942, five months after his presumed death, James Poole was posthumously awarded a Bar to his DSC.

Chapter Thirteen

The Mediterranean Campaign

lso serving in the Mediterranean theatre of war were father and son Charles and Patrick Morgan. Vice-Admiral Charles Morgan, a career sailor, had joined the Royal Navy before the outbreak of the First World War, sailing on HMS *Pelorus* and *Bellona*. He later served as the navigation officer aboard HMS *Caledon*, flagship of the 1st Light Cruiser Squadron, Grand Fleet. Morgan was awarded the Distinguished Service Order (DSO) and promoted to the rank of commander. At the outbreak of the Second World War Captain Morgan was serving as the Royal Navy's Director of Navigation. In November 1940 he was given command of the First World War destroyer HMS *Valiant*, then part of the Mediterranean Fleet under the overall command of Admiral Andrew Cunningham.

Captain Charles Morgan's command ran convoy escort missions in the Mediterranean during the defence of Malta and the campaigns in Greece, Albania and North Africa, facing not only the onslaught of German and Italian surface vessels and dive-bombers but also the ever-present threat of mines and German U-boats in what was one of

Vice-Admiral Sir Charles Morgan KCB, CB, DSO.

the most active theatres of the war for the Royal Navy. Unlike the Italian army and the *Regia Aeronautica*, the Italian fleet (the *Regia Marina*) had been kept up to strength during the inter-war years and now threatened to out-gun the Royal Navy in the theatre. HMS *Valiant* was to play a major role in one of the defining sea battles of the struggle for the Mediterranean when the Royal Navy faced the larger part of the *Regia Marina* under the command of Admiral Angelo Cachino at the Battle of Matapan in the Greek Peloponnese.

The British, however, had one major advantage over the Axis forces. The boffins at Bletchley Park had found a way to break the German codes and so the Royal Navy was able to receive intelligence about the enemy's movements. They knew, for example, that an Italian force composed of one battleship, six heavy and two light cruisers plus escorting destroyers had left port and was nearing Crete, ready to attack a British convoy to the east. The Italians believed there was only one British destroyer in the area and were also unaware of the recent arrival of the aircraft carrier HMS *Formidable*.

In great secrecy Admiral Cunningham left port. Seizing the initiative, he gave orders for his fleet to gather to engage the enemy. On 27 March Vice-Admiral H.D. Pridham-Wippell CB, CVO, RN sailed from Greek waters with the cruisers *Ajax* (Captain E.D.G. McCarthy RN), *Gloucester* (Flag-Captain H.A. Rowley RN), *Orion* (Flag-Captain G.R.B. Back RN) and *Perth* (Captain Sir P.W. Bowyer-Smyth) plus their accompanying destroyers. Meanwhile, Admiral Cunningham with *Formidable* (Captain A.W. La T. Bisset RN), *Warspite* (Flag-Captain D.B. Fisher CBE, RN), *Barham* (Flag-Captain G.C. Cooke RN) and *Valiant* (Captain E.C. Morgan DSO, RN) left Alexandria on the same day to rendezvous with the cruisers.

At 07.55 hours on the 28th the Italian *Trento* group encountered Admiral Pridham-Wippell's cruiser group heading to the south-east. Believing the cruisers were attempting to run away from their larger ships, the Italians gave chase, opening fire at 08.12 hours from 22,000 metres. But the Italian gunners had trouble grouping their rounds and failed to cause any casualties during the hour-long engagement, after which they broke off and turned north-west to rejoin the *Vittorio Veneto*.

Admiral Pridham-Wippell's force continued to shadow the enemy at extreme range. The *Vittorio Veneto*, however, came to the aid of the Italian ships, opening fire on Pridham-Wippell's cruisers from a range of about 23,000 metres at 10.55 hours. Hopelessly out-gunned, the British withdrew with the Italians in pursuit.

HMS *Formidable* had already launched some of its Fairey Albacore torpedo-bombers, which arrived in the nick of time, attacking the *Vittorio Veneto* and forcing her to take avoiding action. As she heeled

Captain Charles Morgan DSO commanded HMS Valiant *at the battle of Matapan on 28 March 1941.* (Reproduced by courtesy of Anne Kennington)

away, her gunners ceased firing on the British cruisers. At 12.20 hours, his attack having lost momentum, Cachino broke off the pursuit. Now aware of the close proximity of a British carrier, he turned towards Taranto and his own air cover.

A second Albacore sortie surprised the Italians at 15.09 hours. Lieutenant Commander Dalyell-Stead broke through the *Vittorio Veneto*'s anti-aircraft fire cordon and dropped a torpedo at close range, damaging the battleship's outer port propeller. Emergency repairs took nearly two hours and *Vittorio Veneto* did not resume her course until 16.42 hours, making 19 knots. On learning of the damage to the Italian battleship, Admiral Cunningham set a course to pursue her.

Meanwhile, *Formidable* launched a third air attack by six Albacores and two Swordfish from 826 and 828 Squadrons, accompanied by two Swordfish from 815 Squadron based on Crete. Hits on the *Pola* crippled the cruiser, forcing her to stop. The *Zara* and *Fiume* were ordered to return and help *Pola*; all were unaware of Cunningham's pursuit. Meanwhile the *Vittorio Veneto* and the other ships continued towards Taranto.

With the light fading, the gunners on the *Vittorio Veneto* were stood down, the Italians still unaware that the Royal Navy ships were drawing ever closer under the cloak of darkness. Radar was still in its infancy, and while the Royal Navy was equipped with basic sets, the Italians relied solely on visual contact to locate Allied shipping; Admiral Cunningham would make the most of this advantage. A night engagement, however, was a gamble, and there remained the possibility of misidentification of radar plots resulting in casualties from 'friendly fire'.

The subsequent naval engagement has been described as 'the most sweeping British naval victory since Trafalgar', and we have Morgan's own account of the encounter:

> *Valiant*'s guns opened fire against the Italian cruiser *Fiume* within seven seconds after the first broadside from *Warspite* struck home. *Valiant*'s shells and those of *Warspite* turned *Fiume* into colossal burst of flames.
>
> She seemed just to burst out amidships. It was the most glorious and at the same time the most ghastly five minutes in my life. Great glows illuminated the darkness from the *Fiume* like someone throwing a log on a fire. The whole ship seemed to disintegrate, many of our shells exploding inside her and turning her into a raging, blazing inferno.

The stricken *Fiume* was put out of action within four minutes of the beginning of the engagement. *Valiant* then blasted away at the *Zara*, with 75 per cent of her shells hitting their target. Hit by some 35 tons of high explosives, *Zara* suffered the same fate as the *Fiume*. Neither ship responded with its own guns, as Morgan recalled:

> There was no replying fire from either *Fiume* or *Zara*. We fired some star-shells to help light up the targets, and the cruisers apparently thought they were flares from aircraft, for they let go some of their guns in the direction of the falling star-shells.

All guns were now turned on the two Italian destroyers *Vittorio Alfieri* and *Giosue*, which were sunk in short order, while the *Gioberti* and *Oriani* were also hit.

In the middle of the battle, Royal Navy ships stopped to pick up survivors. A total of 55 officers and 850 other ratings were hauled aboard before dive-bombers forced the ships to leave the scene. Details of the location of the remaining survivors was sent to the Chief of the Italian Naval Staff, and the Italian hospital ship *Gradisca* was given unhindered passage to rescue them.

In a battle that raged for some twenty minutes the guns of HMS *Valiant*, *Warspite* and *Barham* had sunk three Italian cruisers and two destroyers and seriously damaged several warships, including the greatly prized *Vittorio Veneto*. *Pola* was captured but had to be scuttled. The Italians lost up to 2,303 sailors, most of them from *Zara* and *Fiume*, while the British casualties consisted of three air crew killed on a torpedo-bomber shot down by anti-aircraft gunners on the *Vittorio Veneto*.

The Royal Navy's victory at Matapan was a major defeat for the *Regia Marina*, but for the Allies it offered little more than a brief respite. Greece was lost in April 1942 and a month later the island of Crete was captured by German paratroops. Meanwhile the British fleet was also badly mauled, with only two battleships, three cruisers and thirteen destroyers surviving to protect our convoys. Both HMS *Valiant* and *Queen Elizabeth* were later badly damaged by Italian 'Chariot' two-man torpedoes while they lay in port, further weakening the Royal Navy's surface fleet in the Mediterranean.

Captain Morgan's role at Matapan was recognised with a Mention in Dispatches, and he was promoted to the rank of rear admiral and appointed Flag Officer Commanding Taranto and the Adriatic. He was made a Commander of the Bath (CB) in the New Year's Honours List of 1945.

In 1946 Vice-Admiral Morgan was made a Knight Commander of the Bath (Military Division) and two years later, as the Navy's Liaison Officer, was given the honour of presenting Italian gallantry awards to the Italians who had put HMS *Valiant* and *Queen Elizabeth* out of action. Even more remarkably, Morgan had actually recommended one of the men, Luigi de la Penne, for the British DSO for gallantry at La Spezia after Italy had surrendered and joined the Allies' cause.

Patrick John Morgan DSC

Vice-Admiral Charles Morgan's son Patrick also served in the Mediterranean during the war. He was the navigation officer aboard HMS *Penelope*, which was known throughout the Royal Navy as 'Pepperpot' *Penelope*. Damaged during the Norway campaign of April–May 1940, HMS *Penelope* had undergone repairs and now had a new crew and a new mission too. Under the command of Captain Angus Dacres Nicholl RN, she sailed from Scapa Flow on 12 October 1941 in company with her sister-ship HMS *Aurora* (Captain William Agnew RN) bound for the Mediterranean. They arrived in Malta nine days later.

Serving as part of a raiding squadron named 'Force K', the two cruisers and their escorting destroyers *Lance* (Lieutenant Commander

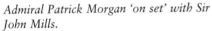

Admiral Patrick Morgan 'on set' with Sir John Mills.

Studio photograph of Admiral Patrick Morgan DSC.

Ralph Northcott RN) and *Lively* (Lieutenant Commander William Hussey RN) were assigned the task of disrupting supplies to Rommel's German *Afrika Korps*. Force K relied on a combination of message intercepts, aerial reconnaissance and good fortune to locate enemy convoys. On 8 November a convoy of six destroyers and ten merchant ships heading for Libya was sighted by the crew of a Maryland reconnaissance aircraft.

Force K duly sailed from Malta as dusk fell, spotting the enemy at 00.45 hours. They also located a second force of Italian heavy cruisers, the convoy's main escort, some 6 miles away. It took fifteen anxious minutes for the British cruisers to draw within firing range, placing the merchantmen and escort 'up moon' and attacking from the starboard quarter. Remarkably neither the convoy nor its escort spotted Force K before *Aurora*'s guns opened fire. The engagement began at 00.57 hours and took place off Cape Spartivento, and later became known as the 'Battle of the Duisburg Convoy'. During the battle, which lasted twenty-five minutes, HMS *Penelope* brought her guns to bear on eleven targets, firing a total of sixty broadsides. Although she was straddled by rounds from the distant escort ships, HMS *Penelope* escaped damage or casualties. The Italians were not so lucky. The Italian destroyer *Fulmine* was sunk, while the *Euro* and *Grecale* were badly damaged. All the merchant ships in the convoy, including a 10,000-ton tanker and a 4,000-ton ammunition ship, were sent to the bottom. In all, Rommel's troops, then besieging the Allies at Tobruk, were denied some 60,000 tons of vital supplies.

Lieutenant Patrick Morgan was awarded the Distinguished Service Cross for his gallantry during the engagement, his award being announced in the *London Gazette* in April the following year: 'For gallantry, skill and resolution in a brilliant night action south of Taranto, against odds, in which, without hurt or loss to the Royal Navy, ten enemy supply ships and a destroyer were sunk, and at least one other badly damaged.'

On 23 November 1941 Force K sailed from Malta to intercept another Axis convoy west of Crete. The vessels spread out to search for the enemy, and it was the crew of HMS *Penelope* who sighted and engaged the convoy at 15.36 hours. Two oil transporters were identified as the Italian *Procida* of 1,842 tons and the German *Maritza* of 2,910 tons, escorted by the destroyers *Cassiopaea* and *Lupo*. Dodging bombs dropped by enemy aircraft, HMS *Penelope* fought a half-hour duel with the destroyers which eventually fled, leaving the merchant vessels to their fate. The crew of HMS *Penelope* received the prime minister's congratulations on their fine work, which had been much publicised in the press and in the Pathé newsreels.

Further success came on 1 December 1941 when *Penelope* and *Aurora* sank the Italian merchant vessel *Adriatico*, as well as the destroyer *Alvise da Mosto* and the stranded tanker *Iridio Mantovani* of 10,540 tons. On 3 December 1941 they were congratulated for their continued successes by the First Sea Lord. Meanwhile, Captain Nicholl received a message from the Mayor of Blackpool saying that the Lancashire seaside town wished to 'adopt' the much-publicised *Penelope* as part of Warship Week.

HMS *Penelope* was in action once again on 16 December. During an eleven-minute action known as the First Battle of Sirte, Force K and the 15th Cruiser Squadron were subjected to air attack by twenty-five enemy torpedo-bombers and fifty Junkers Ju 87s. Remarkably not one Allied vessel was damaged. But Force K's luck was about to change.

HMS *Neptune*, *Aurora* and *Penelope* all struck mines at about 01.00 hours on 19 December while sailing out of Tripoli but only HMS *Neptune* was badly damaged. The Force K commander, Captain Agnew, decided that a destroyer or cruiser could not be risked in the minefield to tow her out, so *Penelope*, *Kandahar* and *Lively* were left to defend the stricken *Neptune* while she waited for a tug to come out from Malta. As they drifted *Neptune* and *Kandahar* hit further mines and *Penelope* was forced to make for Malta, leaving the surviving crew of *Kandahar* to be rescued by HMS *Jaguar* the following evening.

Having undergone repairs, HMS *Penelope* sailed from Valletta on 17 January, rendezvousing with an incoming convoy which she escorted into harbour. The role of convoy escort was to become a regular feature of Force K's work, and on 13 February 1942 HMS *Penelope* left Malta in the company of six destroyers to escort an eastward-bound convoy which included the *Breconshire*. HMS *Penelope* returned to Malta on the 15th, with the destroyers HMS *Lance* and *Legion*.

On 22 March 1942 HMS *Penelope* sailed from Malta to escort another convoy into Valletta. This mission, however, was to be full of incident. The Italians had learned of the convoy's departure from Alexandria from a U-boat stationed off the coast. The Italian Battle Fleet, consisting of the battleship *Littorio* and six destroyers from Taranto, was dispatched to rendezvous with the heavy cruisers *Trento* and *Gorizia*, along with the light cruiser *Bande Nere* and four destroyers from Messina. The plan was for this combined force to intercept and destroy the convoy before it reached Malta.

The Italians successfully placed their fleet in the path of the convoy and its escort, which consisted of Force K and the 5th Destroyer Flotilla. The first attacks came from Italian Savoia SM 79 torpedo-bombers and 150 Junkers Ju 87 dive-bombers; their assault began at 09.30 hours and lasted five-and-a-half hours. The barrels of *Penelope*'s anti-aircraft guns were already red hot when the Italian fleet was sighted and the British 'made smoke' to conceal the destroyers and the convoy from the Italian ships' guns. Shells straddled some of the vessels of the 5th Destroyer Flotilla, but they replied with such accuracy that the Italians withdrew.

A second engagement began at 16.37 hours with the arrival of the main Italian force, including *Littorio*, the eight-inch cruisers *Trento* and *Gorizia*, the six-inch cruiser *Bande Nere* and their destroyer escort. Emerging from the cover of smoke, *Penelope* engaged the *Gorizia* between 17.03 and 17.10 hours, but when *Littorio* returned fire *Penelope* steered back into smoke cover.

Fending off the Italians with salvos of broadsides and torpedoes, the Royal Navy fought with great skill and determination and somehow managed to save the convoy. In one exchange, during the heaviest fighting, HMS *Penelope* had fired thirteen broadsides, warding off the enemy and damaging one enemy cruiser.

Half an hour from Malta's main harbour, however, the *Breconshire* was hit by a bomber. Despite the continuing air attacks, HMS *Penelope* sailed back out of port and came alongside the crippled vessel, helping to fight the fire. Attempts to tow the *Breconshire* into Valletta failed and so members of *Penelope*'s crew returned to her aid with the tugs *Ancient* and *Robust*. After fourteen hours, during which the *Breconshire* and her would-be rescuers were subject to heavy seas and air attack, she was eventually towed as far as Marsaxlokk Bay, where emergency repairs could be made.

Force K's epic and spirited defence of this convoy inspired Churchill to send a congratulatory signal on 23 March:

> I shall be glad if you will convey the admiration which I feel at this resolute and brilliant action by which the Malta convoy was saved. That one of the most powerful modern battleships afloat attended by cruisers and destroyers should have been routed and put to flight in broad daylight by five British light cruisers and destroyers constitutes a naval episode of the highest distinction. It entitles all ranks and ratings concerned and above all their commanders to the compliments of the British nation.

While this convoy may have got through, the siege of Malta had by no means been lifted and there now began a period of intense bombing. HMS *Penelope* was holed both forward and aft by near-misses on 26 March while berthed at Hamilton Wharf in French Creek. One bomb exploded between the ship and the dock-side, rupturing the hull and igniting cordite rounds in the for'ard ammunition store. Luckily, these were immediately extinguished by the inrushing sea water.

Emergency repairs were made to *Penelope* in Valletta's dry dock, with a steel girder being welded to her keel and thick plates covering the great gashes in her hull. Meanwhile, she remained a sitting duck and was subjected to fourteen days of heavy air raids, during which some 3,000 bombs and 14 aerial torpedoes fell on the docks and surrounding area. The ship's gunners fired 70,000 rounds in her defence, and were obliged to replace her worn-out gun barrels. Throughout the raids her decks were showered with rocks and concrete as a result of nearby explosions. The dry dock was partly flooded and then set alight by burning oil from tankers sunk in the harbour. During her last day in Malta *Penelope* was subjected to seven concerted raids by Junkers Ju 87 dive-bombers. By the end of it all, forty-two bomb-craters surrounded her berth but she had suffered no direct hits. Nevertheless, she was peppered with thousands of shrapnel holes from bombs which had exploded within feet of her hull, thus earning her the fond nickname 'Pepperpot' *Penelope*.

On 8 April, with her makeshift repairs completed, HMS *Penelope* slipped out of Malta and into Navy folklore. There was no disguising her intention to head for Gibraltar, and she was repeatedly bombed on the following day. Astonishingly, she arrived unscathed on 10 April. Later that day she received a signal from Vice-Admiral, Malta: 'True to your usual form. Congratulations.' On the following day HMS *Penelope* was visited by HRH the Duke of Gloucester, while the First Sea Lord congratulated the ship on her safe arrival.

Following further temporary repairs, HMS *Penelope* sailed for the American Navy Yard in New York for more extensive work, leaving Gibraltar on 10 May 1942. She was under repair until September, only arriving back at Portsmouth on 1 October 1942.

King George VI held an investiture at Buckingham Palace on 7 December 1943, during which the officers and men of HMS *Penelope* were presented with a number of awards for gallantry, including two Distinguished Service Orders, a Distinguished Service Cross and two Distinguished Service Medals. Among those lining up to receive their awards was Lieutenant Morgan.

Chapter Fourteen

The North Africa Campaign

The Territorials of the QORR had been mobilised on 1 September 1939 and were already at camp at Welbeck Abbey when war was declared two days later. On that fateful morning the Stafford men of 4 Troop, B Squadron, were playing football at 11.00 hours when the game was stopped for all to gather around the radio to listen to Prime Minister Neville Chamberlain's speech.

Members of 4 Troop, B Squadron of the Staffordshire Yeomanry (QORR) at summer camp, 1938.

Under the command of Lieutenant Colonel R.S. Manley TD, the men's training was to intensify, while the regiment, still officially a cavalry unit, prepared for overseas service. Troopers too young for active service were transferred away and the regiment was posted to the Middle East, arriving at Haifa in early January 1940. Italy's declaration of war on 10 June 1940 meant that Palestine became an active war zone.

Members of 4 Troop of the Staffordshire Yeomanry at Patshull in 1938. The regiment remained a cavalry unit until 1941.

The QORR men were stationed to patrol the border with Syria, which came under the control of the Vichy government on 27 June.

Later, the regiment lost its commanding officer, Lieutenant Colonel Manley, who was replaced by Major G.G. Cox-Cox. At the same time Major J.A. Eadie was made second-in-command.

In August 1941 the QORR, now stationed at Hadera, surrendered their horses and received instead American Stuart and Grant tanks. A number of sergeant instructors sent from the Royal Tank Regiment (RTR) helped to turn cavalrymen into drivers, wireless operators, mechanics and gunners. In mid-June 1942 the QORR handed over their tanks to 3/4 City of London Yeomanry, the crews and the echelon reforming at Mareopolis Camp on 26 June. Two months later they were re-equipped, A and B Squadrons receiving Grants, while C Squadron was issued with light reconnaissance Crusader tanks.

Colonel Eadie DSO and Bar. He commanded the Staffordshire Yeomanry during the battle of El Alamein and during the Normandy campaign.

The regiment then moved to El Huweijja, taking up a position on the southern flank of the El Alamein line as a safeguard against an outflanking manoeuvre. On 31 August German

The North Africa Campaign

tanks began advancing along the regiment's front. Major Farquhar led his Crusaders on a reconnaissance sortie, while tanks of the 22nd Armoured Division, on the QORR's flank, successfully engaged the enemy. After this, the QORR advanced to Wadi el Sakran, where they held Bare Ridge against a possible advance. At approximately 09.00 hours the enemy's artillery opened fire, heralding a tank battle that was to last until dusk. During the fighting B Squadron's echelon was bombed by Junkers Ju 87s, while the QORR's gunners knocked out several German tanks and anti-tank guns.

Staffordshire Yeomanry tanks on the move in the Western Desert, 1941.

The following morning saw the enemy retreating, and by 8 September they had pulled back to their original position, except on the southern edge of the El Alamein line, where they remained in advance of their own minefield. Meanwhile, the tanks of the QORR were ordered to fall back in preparation for the main British offensive.

At this time Lieutenant Colonel Cox-Cox was posted away and Colonel Eadie was appointed as the regiment's new commanding officer. Meanwhile, in preparation for Montgomery's offensive, the regiment underwent a rigorous programme of training. The gunners gained valuable time on the firing-ranges, while all the crews went on night manoeuvres with The Buffs and the 1st Regiment, Royal Horse Artillery, during which they worked on breaching minefields.

Montgomery's battle-plan relied partly on convincing his opponent, Field Marshal Ernst Rommel, that the real push would happen elsewhere along the front. Consequently, the formation was dispatched to the southern limits of the line, a known weak spot in the enemy's defences. Once they were observed taking up their positions here, their tanks were replaced by canvas dummies, the real tanks returning under cover of darkness to the northern reaches of the Alamein line, where they were concealed under canvas-covered frames cleverly fashioned to resemble the Army's ubiquitous 3-ton trucks. On the morning of 23 October Colonel Eadie briefed his men on Montgomery's battle-plan. At 19.00 hours the tank crews were to remove the truck frames and make ready to enter the minefield.

Three hours later, at zero hour, the battle began as the thousands of artillery pieces that had been concentrated along the front were brought to bear on the enemy's lines. A total of 200,000 rounds were fired during a five-hour barrage, under cover of which sappers of the Royal Engineers worked to make safe paths through the mines. At 02.00 hours on 24 October the QORR advanced into the gap between the Allied minefields heading for Mitereiya Ridge. Major Farquhar, formerly a trooper with the Stafford Troop, led the regiment's Crusader tanks as they advanced towards the ridge.

Colonel Eadie (second from left) and Field Marshal Montgomery (third from left) discuss the progress of the campaign.

Despite the enemy's losses during the bombardment, the men of the QORR found themselves engaged in a gritty tank battle during which a number of their own tanks were lost. Major Farquhar had three tanks 'brew-up' under his command during the action. Eventually, the

Field Marshal Montgomery viewing the battlefield from the turret of a British tank.

Crusaders were forced to withdraw, Farquhar stopping to rescue a number of crews from the battlefield.

The Germans counter-attacked but the QORR's Grants halted their advance in its tracks, destroying fourteen enemy tanks. Major Meynell's gunner, Sergeant Fuller, accounted for five of them. However, during the engagement Captain Lord Lewisham and Lieutenant Harris's tanks were lost, and at dusk the regiment withdrew to regroup. While attempting to link up with the 24th Armoured Brigade, Lieutenant Guy Matthews had three scout-cars blown up by landmines.

Staffordshire Yeomanry tanks on the move in the North Africa campaign.

Officers of the Staffordshire Yeomanry taking cover under artillery fire.

After a further engagement the QORR finally made a vital breakthrough, capturing the El Wiska Ridge. Advancing still further, the regiment came under terrific fire from a number of German 88mm anti-tank guns, which wreaked havoc among the Grants. With their infantry support forced to fall back, the tanks were left exposed and ten Grants were soon destroyed, resulting in the death of Eadie's second-in-command, Major Wilmot Longstaff. Also killed were Captain Lord Lewisham, Captain Dennis Bennett, Lieutenant Gordon Lock and Lieutenant John Newbiggin.

Battlefield burial of a Staffordshire Yeomanry tank crew somewhere in North Africa, 1942.

The North Africa Campaign

When the QORR regrouped on the Mitereiya Ridge, close to their starting position, they could only muster one squadron, so great had been their losses. Major Eadie ordered the armour to retire to the relative shelter of the Quattara Road in readiness for the next phase of the battle.

The night of 28 October was spent in a forward location ahead of the artillery. In this exposed position the QORR came under fire from the enemy concealed among the battlefield debris. On the following day an attempt was made to recover any serviceable tanks from the minefield.

A new offensive was launched on 2 November, the tanks this time successfully breaching the German minefield. The advance was temporarily halted, however, by 88mm anti-tank guns positioned on the right flank. These guns were taken on by the QORR's Crusader tanks, quickly supported by the heavier Grants. Wheeling on the 2nd Armoured Brigade, the QORR fought a fierce battle in the Tel el Aqqaqir area.

During the following day the QORR engaged enemy tanks and 88mm guns, taking a number of casualties, with Major Himley Cartwright, Captain Chris Nicholls and Captain John Cunliff-Lister all wounded. By 4 November, however, the enemy had withdrawn and the QORR's tanks were able to advance on Birel Abd, where a thousand Axis troops were taken prisoner, the regiment's armoured cars capturing General Thoma, Rommel's second-in-command.

A further disaster befell the Axis forces when a column of Italian tanks simply drove into the British brigade at Gala Station and some 58 M13 tanks were destroyed or captured without loss. Meanwhile, the QORR's Crusaders, under Lieutenant Tiptoft, were sent on ahead and captured Fuka airfield, Tiptoft personally taking the Italians' surrender.

The British advance had resulted in a rout and in late November the QORR tanks were put on transporters and driven past the scene of many earlier deadly conflicts: Sidi Barrani, Tobruk and Benghazi. The regiment's tanks were finally redeployed 8 miles north of Agedabia, and the Crusaders were sent out to reconnoitre Rommel's defences. Meanwhile, A Squadron was attached to the 2nd New Zealand Division and made an outflanking manoeuvre around Rommel's box defence, while the remainder of the regiment joined the brigade in attacking the weakest sector along the front.

On 14 December the QORR advanced and engaged a number of Italian M13s, destroying nearly a dozen, four of them being hit by Lieutenant Manning's troop. By the following morning the enemy had once more retreated. Lieutenant Manning took up the pursuit, finding a place to traverse an anti-tank ditch, and was quickly followed by the remainder of the regiment, which was engaged by heavy artillery. Once again the enemy pulled back under the cover of darkness.

The regiment was then rested in preparation for the advance on the Buerat-Bungem line, leading to an engagement at Wadi Zem Zem. The QORR led the 8th Armoured Brigade in the assault, taking on the 15th Panzers and their supporting 88mm anti-tank guns dug in on the reverse slope. During the bitter engagement that followed, Lieutenant Matthews was killed, while his wireless operator, Trooper Cartwright, gallantly risked his own life to release his trapped driver.

The brigade suffered heavy losses on the left flank of the advance when it became pinned down by 88mm anti-tank guns. The QORR tanks were sent in to give much-needed support but the following day they were harried by Stuka dive-bombers attempting to halt their advance. At Sedada, where the vast expanse of open desert gives way to hilly outcrops and vegetation, the enemy made full use of the terrain to deploy their 88mm anti-tank guns. However, the QORR's tanks successfully took them on without loss.

Meanwhile, a detachment of five Crusaders with artillery support was sent on ahead to block the Tarhuna road, the brigade capturing Tarhuna on 15 January. The Burgomeister surrendered the town to a detachment of the QORR.

Eight days later the 11th Hussars entered Tripoli, while the QORR tanks were ordered to advance on Denzar and later occupied the area around Regdalin, forming a bridgehead for the brigade. The Germans

The tanks of the Staffordshire Yeomanry enter Tripoli.

tried to push the regiment back, but lost several Mark IV Special Tanks in the attempt. The QORR was then deployed to counter a possible break-out by Rommel's tanks but this failed to materialise. However, the regiment was later moved by transporter to Bir Sultane, where it was again in action on 22 March 1943. Although the tank-on-tank battle was won, the regiment was heavily shelled and bombed over the next few days and suffered some losses.

On 26 March the QORR took part in the major advance towards El Hamma. The battle that followed was a fierce and costly one, resulting in the destruction of a number of enemy tanks. Colonel Eadie was slightly wounded when an armour-piercing shell passed through his tank. He was relieved by Major I.A. Spence for two days before resuming command.

The regiment was in action once more on 5 April, when the brigade advanced up Wadi Akarit. The ensuing tank battle saw the QORR's armour coming up against German Tiger tanks for the first time; they destroyed one and forced the remainder into retreat. The following day the Germans counter-attacked on the regiment's open flank, attempting a hook manoeuvre. Colonel Eadie immediately deployed his armour and ordered a concentrated fire on the enemy, which destroyed a number of German tanks and quickly halted the advance.

Moving on to the south of Enfidaville, the regiment was once more to find itself fighting against German armour and heavy artillery. Major Cunliff-Lister was hit and later died of his wounds. The regiment suffered from heavy shelling over the next few days and was unable to make any headway against the enemy, who held strong positions in the nearby hills.

The advance on the hill outposts and coastal track protected by 88mm anti-tank guns began on 9 May. Within four days, however, all resistance had virtually melted away and the Allies entered Tunis.

The QORR had advanced some 1,850 miles from their starting point on the El Alamein front, traversing every kind of terrain and under extreme conditions: at night a man could almost freeze to death while during the day he could be dead in a matter of hours from heat exhaustion and dehydration in temperatures hot enough to fry an egg on a tank's armour plate. The victory was a tribute to the incalculable bravery of the tank crews and maintenance units, who serviced the tanks and vehicles despite the sandstorms and without a regular supply of spares. What was more remarkable was the fact that the QORR had done all this without direct infantry support.

Chapter Fifteen

241st Field Battery (Stafford Battery), Royal Artillery

Embodied on 2 September 1939 under the command of Major W.H. Westhead, the Stafford Battery became part of the newly consolidated 59th (Midlands) Division (the Pithead Division). Following mobilisation at Stafford, the Battery transferred to Burton-on-Trent in October 1939, remaining there for five months. Here Major K.M. Wright assumed temporary command. The Battery was not, however, sent to join the BEF and so surrendered its four 18-pounder field-guns to 116th Field Regiment, Royal Artillery, receiving in their place two obsolete 4.5-inch howitzers intended for drill purposes only.

A Troop, Stafford Battery, 1945.

With the threat of invasion ever-present during the latter half of 1940, the Stafford Battery was deployed on coastal defence duties at Scarborough, later moving to Sandsend and then to Redcar. Following annual camp at Catterick in October 1940, the Battery received a succession of postings to Barnard Castle, Bishops Auckland and Haltwhistle, before moving to Northern Ireland.

In September 1939 the battery had been almost exclusively composed

B Troop, Stafford Battery, 1945.

of Staffordians. Under wartime conditions, however, a percentage of the unit's strength was posted away. The process began in early 1940, when the Stafford Battery lost its CO, Lieutenant Colonel L.H. Morris, along with Captains O. Roberts and D. Morris, and about twenty of the other ranks who were exchanged with personnel from the 10th Field Regiment. Another batch of Staffordians left with Captain Riley in order to form 443rd Field Battery, RA. Meanwhile, C Battery, formed in April 1939 to include clerks, draughtsmen and surveyors, lost its pre-war designation as the 'Businessman's Battery'. Lieutenant Colonel E.B. Smith became the new CO, while second-in-command Major Wright was replaced by Captain R.J.C. Evans, who later commanded the Battery from 1942 until 1945.

The Battery remained on Home Defence duties until 1944, when the Pithead Division took a leading role in the invasion of north-west Europe, training for which had begun in England the previous year. Following a final practice camp at Redesdale in April 1944, the Stafford Battery was stationed at St Lawrence College, Ramsgate, ready for the invasion to begin. With their vehicles waterproofed and extra rations and new equipment issued, all the men knew that it would not be long before they were in action as a part of the amphibious force bound for somewhere along the French coast. Their nervous excitement was reinforced by a morale-boosting visit from General Montgomery.

D-Day came and went, however, and it was not until 23 June that the Battery disembarked from the *Houston City* bound for Le Hamel. Arriving ahead of the remainder of the 177th Brigade, which formed part of the 59th Division, the Battery was temporarily deployed to assist the Canadians in assaulting a position near Carpiquet aerodrome. The battle was hard-fought, the aerodrome being heavily defended with well dug-in machine-gun nests and mortars. As more of the 59th Division landed, the Stafford Battery was reassigned to assist the 5th South Staffs. in blocking any potential German break for the beaches.

The Battery's first major action began with the belated advance on Caen, code-named operation 'Charnwood'. Tanks of the 21st Panzer Division, reinforced by those of the 12th SS Hitlerjugend (Hitler Youth), lay to the north of Caen, stopping the British and Canadians in their tracks. Montgomery, fearful of growing losses, made an outflanking manoeuvre to the west, later deploying the tanks of the 7th Armoured Division, including the QORR.

Operation 'Epsom', an offensive between Caen and Tilly-sur-Seulles, was launched in late June and the Odon was successfully crossed on 27 June. Then the advance was brought to an abrupt halt by two SS armoured divisions near Hill 112.

Montgomery was forced to make a direct assault on Caen, which had by now become the linchpin of the whole front. Two objectives of the main attack on 8 July were Galamanche, to be taken by 2/6th South Staffs. Regiment, supported by 241st Battery, and La Bijude, which was to be taken by the rest of the 6th North Staffs. Regiment. Galamanche proved to be a tough objective. The small chateau, with its outbuildings heavily fortified with trenches and gun emplacements, was defended mightily by the 12th SS Hitlerjugend. The Stafford Battery was ordered to give close support to the advancing 2/5th Lancashire Fusiliers. However, due to confusion in the 'fog of war', a signal was sent to both units stating that both Galamanche and La Bijude had been taken. As the Fusiliers advanced on nearby Malan, they were caught out in the open by fire from positions they believed had already been captured.

During the engagement Gunner F. Clewley moved forward under heavy fire, relaying the enemy's co-ordinates and raining down suppressing fire on their guns. Clewley's actions undoubtedly prevented many casualties and he was later awarded the French Croix de Guerre for his gallantry. Elsewhere, the British front line pushed towards the outskirts of Lébisey, matching the furthest advances made by the QORR a whole month earlier on D-Day.

The Germans were on the run for the first time since the invasion, and that evening they began to retreat. On the following morning the Canadians captured Carpiquet, St-Germain-la-Blanche-Herbe, Venoix

241st Field Battery (Stafford Battery), Royal Artillery

Bombardier S.T. Chilton (left) of the Stafford Battery, RA, and Private N.H.P. Davies (right) of the Wiltshire Regiment were awarded a General Montgomery Certificate for their gallantry in north-west Europe.

and La Maladrerie. At long last the Allies entered the ruined city of Caen, one of their D-Day objectives.

Later the Stafford Battery gave support to the 2/6th South Staffs. at the Orne bridgehead, and saw further action during the advance through north-west Europe, first during operation 'Pomegranate', the advance on Noyers (16–18 July), and later during the crossing of the river Orne north of Thury-Harcourt (6–10 August). The 59th Division was to play a part in the closing of the Falaise Gap (11–17 August), the Stafford Battery later laying a barrage on the area around the river Schelt near Antwerp in advance of the swimming tanks of the QORR.

In February 1945 the Stafford Battery converted to 240mm guns and was redesignated as 241st Super-Heavyweight Battery, RA. Returning into combat in time for the crossing of the Rhine, the gunners later laid down a three-hour barrage in readiness for the crossing of the river Rees. There then followed the battle of Leer and the advance on Emden.

Fighting with distinction throughout the liberation of Europe, the men of the Stafford Battery won a total of twenty awards for gallantry under enemy fire. The campaign, however, cost the lives of Captain Burns, Bombardier Ellis, and Gunners Lockett and Thomas.

Stafford at War

The Stafford Battery's roll of gallantry awards:

OBE	Captain G.W. Riley
MC and Bar	Temporary Major D. Morris
MM	Lance-Bombardier L.T. Dunlop
Croix de Guerre	Gunner S.T. Clewley
Czech Military Cross	Temporary Major A.L.P. Sandy
	Temporary Captain S.F. Smith
Mention in Dispatches	Temporary Major R.J.C. Evans
	Temporary Captain G.R. Lewin
	Temporary Captain S.F. Smith
	BQSM A. Turner
	Bombardier S.T. Chilton
	Bombardier H.W. Sully
	Gunner P.H. Barnes
	Gunner J.N. Boseley
Commander-in-Chief's Certificate for Gallantry	Lieutenant G.E.M. Barnes
	Bombardier S.T. Chilton
	Bombardier R. Wagg
	Gunner G. Burgess
Commander-in-Chief's Certificate for Good Conduct	Sergeant W.H. Yates
	WO 2nd Class W. Whitehead

Chapter Sixteen

A Polish SOE Agent's Story

The Special Operations Executive (SOE) was formed in July 1940 in the wake of the occupation of the greater part of Europe by the Axis powers and their temporary ally, Stalinist Russia. Its aim was to support resistance movements behind enemy lines and, as Winston Churchill put it, to 'set Europe ablaze'. The Polish resistance made perhaps the greatest contribution to the outcome of the war by secretly capturing a German Enigma encoding machine and smuggling it to England. Using this machine the brilliant code-breakers at Bletchley Park were able to supply Britain's High Command with details of Germany's battle-plans within days, if not hours, of the initial radio intercept. Without this highly sophisticated technology, the German U-boats would have gone unchecked and the RAF would not have had advanced warning of many air raids during the Battle of Britain.

At first the Polish Resistance movement, known as the Home Army or Armia Krajowa (AK), was isolated from the Polish Government in Exile, which was based in London. Messages sent by couriers from its headquarters in Warsaw took too long to arrive, while the journey was extremely perilous. The first Polish officers were dropped into their homeland on the night of 15/16 February, a Whitley bomber making the dangerous 14-hour flight via the North Sea, southern Denmark and the Baltic. Their prime task was to 'maintain liaison with the home country'. In the course of the war there would be a total of 485 drops into Poland, 192 of them to Warsaw and its environs. In all, 316 agents and trained combatants were parachuted into enemy-occupied Poland, of whom 120 were killed by the Germans or Russians. A further 28 couriers also made the highly dangerous journey.

The conquest of southern Italy in the summer of 1944 gave the RAF a new route into Poland and led to the SOE establishing a command centre near Bari in southern Italy. Halifax bombers and American Liberators were flown on supply and agent drops by 624 (Special Duties) Squadron and 1386 (Polish) Flight. These missions were among the most dangerous ever flown by the Allies; in an attempt to supply the AK during the Warsaw Rising, fifteen out of the sixteen aircraft dispatched failed to return.

One of those who served with the SOE in Poland, and who fought under the command of the Polish Government in Exile, was Zdzislaw Luszowicz, who was temporarily billeted at former RAF Wheaton Aston Polish Resettlement Camp in 1946 and later made Stafford his home.

Born in the ancient city of Cracow in southern Poland on 26 June 1914, Zdzislaw completed one year's compulsory military service as a cadet officer in September 1938 and in August 1939 joined his unit, 20th Infantry, for their annual manoeuvres, scheduled to end on 3 September. However, on 1 September the Germans attacked Poland, crossing the border not far from where Zdzislaw's regiment was stationed. His unit was in combat within two hours of the opening of hostilities. The German Panzer divisions had invaded his country 'in defence' of Hitler's Third Reich. Members of the Wehrmacht dressed in Polish uniforms made a 'raid' on a German radio station just over the Polish/German border, thus justifying any act of 'retribution' against Poland. Poland's fate was sealed, however, on 17 September when, in accordance with the terms of the secret Ribbentrop-Molotov Pact, the Russians invaded eastern Poland. A lack of weapons and ammunition led to Zdzislaw's unit being ordered to surrender to the Russians on 22 September.

A former officer cadet, Zdzislaw's commission had finally come through, being announced in the daily orders but not yet published. So he was separated from his brother officers and put with the NCOs and other ranks. This undoubtedly saved his life as the Polish officers were later murdered by the Russians during April–May 1940, and their bodies buried in the Katyn Forest.

In July 1941 Hitler launched Operation 'Barbarossa', the invasion of Russia, his former ally. The Polish Government in Exile, then unaware of the Katyn atrocity, made an agreement with Stalin whereby former servicemen and women were released to form an underground army to fight in Poland. Zdzislaw Luszowicz was one of those who volunteered for active service against the Nazis. In August 1941 he became a member of the 18th Infantry Regiment, which formed part of the 6th (Lvov) Division.

This new army, commanded by General Wladyslaw Anders, left Russia via Iran and Iraq, and eventually reached England, where Zdzislaw volunteered for active service with the AK.

Having completed the lengthy recruitment process, Zdzislaw was sent to train at the SOE's fieldcraft training camp or 'station'. The main training centre was at Audley End (Station 43). There he underwent an intensive programme, beginning with a four-week course covering marksmanship, street fighting and the first principles of handling mines. There were, running concurrently with this, daily physical fitness exercises. Many volunteers fell at the first hurdle, so tough was this regime.

There then followed a five- to eight-week course in clandestine activities, on the completion of which the agents focused on sabotage, communications, intelligence and propaganda techniques; Zdzislaw was to specialise in propaganda. Part of the course also involved a mock interrogation at night – the SOE had to have men and women who would not crack even under extreme pressure and violence. The agents were to be dropped into the heart of occupied Poland by parachute, and so, after preliminary work in 'Monkey Grove' in Scotland, they were sent to the parachute training camp at Ringway, making at least eight jumps before being awarded their wings.

Having completed his SOE training, Zdzislaw was then given instruction on using the Polish wireless transmitter and the AK's own ciphers, which were considered unbreakable. While awaiting his first mission into Poland, Zdzislaw learned of the deaths of General Sikorski, the Polish leader in exile, and of the AK's commander in the field, General Stefan Rowecki. These were major losses for the Polish forces. A further blow came in April 1943 with the discovery of the Katyn Forest massacre, perpetrated by the Russians who by now were backing the pro-Communist Armia Ludowa (AL) in Poland.

In the spring of 1944 the Red Army began its advance into Poland. It would approach Warsaw by the late summer, calling on the Polish resistance to create a second front in the city. The Warsaw Rising began on 1 August 1944 and was to be one of the bloodiest battles of the war in the west. But although Russian troops were within artillery range of the Germans in the suburbs, they deliberately left the AK to its fate, refusing even to allow the British or Americans to use Russian airspace to drop supplies; Stalin wanted the AK destroyed, having already decided that after the war Poland would be part of his new Communist Bloc.

It was under these difficult circumstances that Zdzislaw Luszowicz, codenamed Jackal, would be parachuted into the crucible of war. On 4 May 1944 a Halifax bomber of 1386 (Polish) Flight took off from Brindisi in southern Italy bound for Poland. Zdzislaw was one of six agents on board.

Having parachuted into Poland, Zdzislaw linked up with other resistance workers to attack German trains, convoys and installations. His main role was in propaganda and other subversive actions, his job being to raise the morale of his countrymen. In an occupied country every act of defiance was important. Equally, each act carried terrible risks.

Having survived many skirmishes with the Germans, and fought during the defence of Lublin, the Russians overran his sector and Zdzislaw once again came up against the Communist forces, to whom he was betrayed by their Polish sympathisers. 'Jackal' was arrested by Lieutenant Swiatlo of the NKVD, who later became a colonel in Department 10 before defecting to the West and gaining immunity for his previous crimes. During the months that Zdzislaw spent at Stalingorsk Labour Camp he was repeatedly beaten and interrogated, but despite his ordeal he refused to betray the rest of his cell.

Having successfully convinced the Russians that he posed no threat, Zdzislaw was released and returned to Poland. From here he escaped to Italy via Czechoslovakia and Germany. He briefly resumed his post-war career as a teacher before making his way to England, where he was demobilised. Zdzislaw was sent to the Polish Resettlement Camp at Wheaton Aston, where he taught the children of fellow Poles. For his part in Poland's struggle against the Nazis and Communism, Zdzislaw was awarded the King's Medal for Courage in the Cause of Freedom. This medal was the highest gallantry award bestowed on non-British nationals for service in the SOE.

SOE agent Captain Zdzislaw Luszowicz was awarded the King's Medal for Courage in the Cause of Freedom.

Home Army parachutist's badge awarded to Captain Zdzislaw Luszowicz, code-name 'Jackal'.

Chapter Seventeen

Bomber Command

Cheerful Confidence of Brave Bomber Pilot

Since Fighter Command's victory during the Battle of Britain, the fight had been taken to the enemy with sustained night-bombing raids on German industry and infrastructure. Bomber Command was to suffer 55,000 casualties during the campaign, while many more of its men were wounded or taken prisoner.

Among the Staffordians who flew with Bomber Command were a number of former pupils of King Edward VI's Grammar School, including Eric Johnson BEM, DFC, AFC. Eric Johnson passed his schools certificate in June 1938 and became a junior clerk in the Stafford Corporation Treasurer's department. Following the outbreak of war he volunteered as air crew in the RAF but had to wait until a vacancy occurred in May 1941.

Squadron Leader Eric Johnson BEM, DFC, AFC.

Following flying training, and now with the rank of sergeant, Eric was awarded his pilot's brevet on 13 February 1942, and was sent to an Operational Training Unit (OTU) where he converted on to Wellington bombers. On 6 August 1942 he was posted to 427 (Lion) Squadron, Royal Canadian Air Force (RCAF).

Seconded to 419 Squadron, Eric's first mission was an uneventful raid to Turin. Soon afterwards he returned to 427 Squadron, fitting into a crew that already had twelve to fifteen operational flights to its credit. His good fortune continued with the squadron being allocated easier raids before he had to face the daunting task of a mission deep into Germany.

A little light relief came to the pilots of Lion Squadron with a visit from the managing director of Metro-Goldwyn-Mayer, the film-making concern whose trademark was a lion. As Eric Johnson chalked the name of one of the studio's most glamorous stars, Lana Turner, on the side of the wing commander's Halifax, below an image of the reclining superstar, he was caught by a film crew and the image appeared in the Pathé News.

Recommencing operations on Halifax Mark V bombers at Leeming in May 1943, Eric took part in some ten sorties during the Battle of the Ruhr. The high casualty rate at this time meant that only 15 per cent of crews could expect to finish a tour of duty (thirty operational flights). During one week in June 1943 Eric carried out five raids, including one to Mulheim on 22/23 June when his squadron lost four out of seven aircraft dispatched. During this period Eric's original Canadian crew completed their tours and three of them were awarded the Distinguished Flying Cross.

Eric Johnson is seen here receiving his Distinguished Flying Cross from King George VI on 10 December 1943.

Soon after his last Ruhr trip Eric was commissioned as a pilot officer. Following four sorties to Hamburg, he flew his thirtieth mission on the night of 9/10 August 1943 with a raid on Mannheim. He was the first pilot of 247 Squadron to complete a tour; by this date the unit had lost no fewer than twenty-four crews killed or captured.

On 14 September 1943 came the news of his award of the DFC, followed by promotion to the rank of flying officer. The citation read: 'An experienced captain of aircraft, Pilot Officer Johnson has completed many sorties over heavily-defended targets in Germany – his dogged determination and cheerful confidence have been an inspiration to all who have flown with him.' His medal was presented to him by King George VI, who, on pinning the cross to Eric's uniform, asked how long he had been in this country. Eric was, of course, flying with a Canadian squadron, but wore the appropriate 'Great Britain' shoulder flashes. Eric politely explained that he was born here, earning an immediate apology from the King.

Eric Gosling

Another Staffordian with Bomber Command was Warrant Officer Eric Gosling, who served with 102 and 78 Squadrons. Eric was born in Rickerscote, Stafford, where his father was a tenant farmer under T.E. Follows. He enlisted in the RAFVR prior to the war but was not called up until August 1940. Having gone through six weeks' basic training, he went to Fighter Command as an engineer servicing Merlin engines on the legendary Supermarine Spitfire. This work took him to RAF

Tangmere, Hornchurch and Digby. In late 1942 Eric came a step closer to his dream of flying when he was selected for air crew training, becoming a cadet flight engineer. After successfully completing his course, Eric was sent to an OTU flying Halifax bombers. He took part in a number of diversionary raids before flying over northern France on an operational bombing mission.

Eric's first operational posting came in November 1942, when he was sent to 102 (Ceylon) Squadron, later transferring to 78 (Preston) Squadron. He flew on bombing raids to Wuppental, Gelsenkirchen and Dusseldorf. Most daunting of all were the missions to Berlin, which was protected by a network of Luftwaffe night-fighter squadrons and thousands of anti-aircraft batteries.

Eric Gosling was shot down twice while flying with Bomber Command. The second time he became a prisoner of war.

Sergeant Gosling was shot down twice, the first time on 10 July 1943 when his Halifax was hit by flak while on a raid to Gelsenkirchen. The aircraft was caught in the beams of a searchlight and came under intensive fire. The pilot corkscrewed to try to evade the blinding light and the guns it inevitably attracted, but the bomber received several direct hits. Pressing on to the target with one engine dead, the Halifax dropped its payload and plotted a course for home. One bomb, however, failed to release.

Trailing smoke and limping back towards England, the stricken Halifax was easy prey for German night-fighters and, despite the crew taking evasive action and putting up fierce return fire, it sustained further damage and the pilot was forced to ditch out at sea. The incident, which earned Eric a Mention in Dispatches, was later dramatised for BBC radio.

Later in the war Eric took part in the famous Peenemunde raid of 18/19 August 1943. The target was the development site for Hitler's V1 and V2 rockets. The factories and testing-grounds were photographed earlier that year by Staffordian Donald W. Steventon, flying a Photo-Reconnaissance Mosquito. Steventon, a former pupil of King Edward VI Grammar School, won the Distinguished Flying Cross in 1941 and by 1943 had also been awarded the Distinguished Service Order and was commanding 541 Squadron, flying out of RAF Benson.

Eric Gosling was shot down a second time on 15 February 1944, while flying over Rostock heading for Berlin. This time his Halifax disintegrated in mid-air and Eric was thrown clear. Sadly, the rest of the crew, all great friends, perished. A telegram arrived at his mother's house on the following day announcing that Eric was posted as 'missing'. As luck would have it, his name was read out on German radio the following evening. The British made representations via the Red Cross and on 29 March 1944 official confirmation came through that he was being held as a prisoner of war.

Moved from one camp to another, Eric met up with fellow Staffordian Geoff Hall of 427 Squadron while in Stalag 357. Hall had been shot down on his first mission. Both men were liberated by the British 7th Army on 16 April 1945.

Sergeant Roy Hill

Sergeant Roy Hill was a member of 395 (Stafford) Squadron of the ATC and later served as an air gunner on Lancaster bombers with 524 Squadron, Bomber Command. Sadly, Roy was killed in action while flying as 'Tail-end-Charlie' in Lancaster DS 836 on the ill-fated Nuremburg raid.

The raid that cost his crew their lives was launched on the night of 30/31 March 1944. It proved to be the most costly of the entire war in terms of RAF losses, with nearly a hundred bombers lost to anti-aircraft guns and night-fighters, some of which shot down five aircraft in a single sortie. Many aircraft were blown off their true course and bombed other cities around Nuremburg, while other crews dropped their bombs short due to a phenomenon known as 'creep back', as successive crews released their payloads on the previous bombers' explosions rather than on their navigator's plot.

Roy's squadron had been stood down from their two previous missions. As the evening of 30 March drew near they could only guess as to their destination. There were clues, however, as they had seen the ground crews removing part of the previous night's bomb-load and adding more fuel; it was evidently going to be a longer trip, maybe to Berlin.

Gathered in 524 Squadron's briefing room at Waterbeach aerodrome sat an array of pilots, navigators and flight engineers, all awaiting their instructions. The briefing began at 19.50 hours, with the announcement of the target and route. There was a mixture of relief and amazement: relief that it wasn't Berlin, but amazement that they were being ordered to fly straight and level for a staggering 280 miles through the heart of enemy-occupied Europe.

In fact the target was only selected on the morning of the raid, simply because it was Nuremberg's turn. This meant it was far too late for the proper process of target evaluation to take place. The mission was doomed from the start, not least because a faulty radio in one of the Mosquito

Pathfinders meant that it was set permanently on transmit, which resulted in the enemy night-fighters' controllers having a running commentary on events from the moment the bomber force crossed the coast to when they landed.

Preparing for their fourteenth mission was the crew of Avro Lancaster code DS 836, old hands by now: Sergeant D. Crombie (Pilot); Sergeant J. McGahey (Flight Engineer); Pilot Officer Kelly (Navigator); Sergeant M.T. Tyler (Wireless Operator); Sergeant McPhee (Bomb Aimer); Flight Sergeant C. Payne (Mid-Upper Gunner); and Sergeant R. Hill (Rear Gunner).

As the Lancaster taxied ready to take its turn on the main runway, weather conditions over France and Germany were changing

Sergeant Roy Hill, who served in the war as an air gunner.

dramatically, and for the worse. The forecast low cloud had disappeared, while the broken cloud was well above 19,000 feet, the altitude at which the crews were to fly. Disastrously, temperature and atmospheric conditions at that height combined to produce 300-yard-long contrails off the wingtips, which could be seen for many miles in the light of the half-moon, leading prowling night-fighters straight to each bomber. Under these conditions the 280-mile straight flight to Nuremburg would be tantamount to suicide.

Roy watched aircraft after aircraft fall out of the sky as he sat isolated in his turret. That night he saw as many as twenty-five bombers being shot down, giving his pilot a running commentary on each loss. He felt it was only a matter of time before another rear gunner somewhere out there in the formation would be giving the same sort of commentary as Roy's own Lancaster fell out of the sky in a ball of flames. One can only imagine the horrors of that last flight as Roy Hill sat for hour after hour in a death-trap, the loneliest man in the world, eyes straining to see the faint silhouette of the German fighters before they pounced.

So cramped were the conditions in the rear gun turret that Roy was unable to wear a parachute. Instead it had to be stored in a compartment in the main fuselage. The turret was operated by hydraulics. If the hydraulic lines were damaged or the aircraft were thrown about as it descended, then there would be little chance of escape.

As the mission progressed, Sergeant Hill's Lancaster turned southwards heading for Schweinfurt. It was 00.40 hours on the morning

An Avro Lancaster. Roy Hill's gunnery position was in the rear turret, where there was no room for him to wear his parachute.

of 31 March. Kelly had calculated their position based on incorrect data passed on to the crews during the flight, and, like more than a hundred other aircraft, they headed off-course towards the wrong target. The Germans, however, soon spotted the course change and notified their fighter pilots to follow the bomber stream.

With the burning city in sight, a German night-fighter latched on to Roy Hill's Lancaster. Suddenly the aircraft shuddered as cannon fire ripped open the fuselage and the bomber disintegrated in mid-air as 7 tons of high-octane petrol and high explosives erupted in a massive fireball. Miraculously both the bomb-aimer, Sergeant McPhee, and the navigator, Pilot Officer Kelly, were thrown clear by the explosion and managed to pull their rip-cords to deploy their parachutes. Both landed safely and were taken prisoner. Sadly, the remaining members of the crew, including Roy Hill, were all killed; they have no known grave.

The Stafford Squadron of the ATC was later renamed 395 (Roy Hill) Squadron, in memory of the brave air gunner. His proud mother was present at the rededication ceremony.

Training for War
April 1944 saw Trevor Myatt, another former member of the Stafford ATC, flying Vickers Armstrong Wellingtons with an OTU. In fact Trevor's flying career nearly ended before he had flown a single combat mission. On a training flight one morning the bomber he was flying in plummeted out of the sky and crashed soon after take-off. His pilot later reported a sudden loss of power from both engines.

The aircraft lay in a crumpled mass but the fuselage remained largely intact. Trevor and another crew member followed the crash-drill and raced to turn off the fuel taps in order to prevent a fire. The engines, however, had caught alight almost immediately, while the fuel lines themselves were ruptured and were spewing out highly inflammable aviation fuel.

Making his way towards the astrodome, Trevor found his escape route tightly screwed into position. Looking forward, he saw only sheets of flames, while to the rear the floor hatch was jammed against the ground. With no other means of escape, and the heat of the flames pushing him back, he scrambled his way towards the rear gun-turret. With the remainder of his crew safe but too dazed to understand Trevor's plight, he found himself alone in the turret which was facing inwards as the rear gunner had already half rotated it in order to make good his own escape. Trevor turned to face the flames as they crept towards him, blobs of molten metal dripping off the airframe.

Trevor Myatt earned the Distinguished Flying Medal for helping a wounded crew-member into a parachute and evacuating him from their burning aircraft. (Reproduced by courtesy of Anne Kennington)

Meanwhile, Corporal Ernest Leslie Bond, an airman from the station, had seen the Wellington crash and was the first rescuer on the scene. He had already helped the rear gunner out of his turret and now heard Trevor's shouts. Corporal Bond manhandled the gun turret until it faced dead astern, allowing Trevor to climb into it. He then attempted to turn the turret to port but it wouldn't move. The brave corporal shouted instructions to Trevor, telling him how to turn the turret manually so that the escape hatch faced outwards, allowing him to leap to freedom ahead of the flames. The aircraft was rocked by an explosion but Bond stuck to the job, grabbing Trevor's harness once he was free of the turret and dragging him to safety. Corporal Bond was later awarded the British Empire Medal (*London Gazette*, 20 October 1944).

Unbelievably, Trevor and his crew were back in the air within hours of the near-disaster. As they took off in another Wellington, they climbed up over the still-smouldering wreckage.

Trevor completed his training and was flying bombing missions soon after D-Day. Early the following year he was awarded the Distinguished Flying Medal for assisting an injured member of his crew to bale out of their stricken aircraft.

Chapter Eighteen

Coastal Command

Among the largely unsung heroes of the RAF were the air crews of Coastal Command. Their role often involved flying for hours through all weathers in an apparently endless search for enemy surface vessels and U-boats that threatened Allied convoys. One of the many men who undertook this role was a Staffordian, Flight Sergeant Harold Chester. A campanologist at St Mary's Church, Harold trained as a wireless operator but remustered as a trainee pilot, learning to fly in Canada under the Empire Training Scheme.

By June 1943 Harold was with 5 OTU, the last stage before serving with his first operational squadron. On 31 July he was posted to the newly formed 518 Squadron, flying Halifax VI bombers. He later moved to 517 Squadron at St Eval before transferring to 228 Squadron on 28 February 1944.

Based at Pembroke Dock, Harold flew on anti-submarine and anti-shipping patrols, mainly over the Bay of Biscay. The squadron's missions intensified during April and May, as plans for the counter-invasion were put into action. Throughout June 228 Squadron flew increasingly arduous sorties, recording 914 operational hours, keeping the U-boat menace at bay, and providing safe corridors for the D-Day invasion fleet and its supply ships. Thanks to their tireless efforts, not a single cargo ship was lost in June.

Twice in June, on the 5th and again on the 7th, Harold's crew spotted and engaged German U-boats on the surface but return fire from the submarines proved so intense that they were unable to sink them. A few days later Sergeant Chester's crew made another attack: it would be their last act of the war. The story was later recalled by former U-boat Commander Peter E. Cremer Thursby:

> On the night of 11/12 June I was obliged to come to the surface because my batteries were empty. Two aircraft were in the air at a height of about 1,600 feet. I was unable to dive and so was forced to remain on the surface and wait for the attack. My 20mm and 37mm guns were damaged during an earlier engagement, leaving only one twin 20mm gun operational.

Suddenly one of the aircraft attacked at very low altitude. I would guess that it was at 50 feet. The Sunderland was starting to shoot at us with all of its guns at a distance of about 500 yards. Things looked bad for us. Having only one working gun, I started to shoot at a range of about 50 yards at which distance it was impossible to miss him. I hit the starboard engine, which immediately caught fire.

The Sunderland's bullets were piercing our conning tower and oil tanks which began leaking. Amazingly no one was wounded. Meanwhile the Sunderland was losing height and nearly hit the conning tower as it over-flew, missing us by no more than three feet. As it flew past the rear gunner fired concentrated bursts into the submarine then the aircraft crashed into the sea and exploded as a result of the depth-charges it carried. The sea was burning all around us, a mixture of our own oil and fuel from the Sunderland.

There were no survivors of the Sunderland crash. Its own depth-charges ripped it to pieces when it hit the water, and nothing remained to mark the crash-site other than a pool of burning aviation fuel and oil. The bodies of the crew were never recovered and Flight Sergeant Harold Chester is remembered on the Runnymede Memorial.

Chapter Nineteen

Fighter Command

Gallantry and Devotion to Duty

While Fighter Command will always remain synonymous with the Battle of Britain, its pilots played a major role in all theatres of the war.

The Battle of El Alamein, like the events of the summer of 1940, would be a turning point in the war. Churchill later summed up the significance of the battle saying that 'before El Alamein we never had a victory. After El Alamein we never had a defeat.' Two Staffordians played a significant part in the air campaign to protect the 'Alamein Box': Joe Willshaw and Maurice Smyth. Both were later awarded gallantry medals.

War was declared not long after Joe Willshaw's 18th birthday. He enlisted in the RAFVR and in May 1941 was selected for pilot training. Subsequently Flight Sergeant Willshaw was posted to 80 Squadron, stationed in North Africa, arriving at Gambut airfield near Tobruk just as the third German offensive was threatening the front; as a result it was not long before the squadron retreated to Sidi Barrani.

Joe's first operational flight came on 6 June 1942, when he was scrambled to 22,000 feet to attack a group of enemy fighter-bombers; his war had begun in earnest. With the British troops forced eastwards, 80 Squadron fell back to Amriya near El Alamein, where they would hotly defend the El Alamein line,

Joe Willshaw became a fighter ace while serving in North Africa, later winning the DFC as a photo-reconnaissance pilot over Normandy and the Low Countries in 1944. (Reproduced by courtesy of Anne Kennington)

flying almost non-stop during some phases of the battle. Throughout August the heavy air battles continued, with the squadron being regularly scrambled to intercept enemy aircraft or to provide air-to-ground support.

Fighter Command

A sketch of Joe Willshaw's Hawker Hurricane when he was serving with 80 Squadron in the Western Desert in 1941.

Having survived many aerial duels virtually unscathed, Joe was to have a narrow escape on 3 September when his Hawker Hurricane was pounced on by Messerschmitt Bf 109s, one of which got on to his tail. Through skill, training and a measure of good fortune Joe managed to shake the enemy fighters off and made his way back to base.

Joe was soon transferred to 127 Squadron and joined his new unit near Cairo, later moving to an airstrip directly behind the El Alamein front; here the pilots were soon to experience some of the fiercest action of the campaign. For the next few weeks Joe Willshaw flew nearly continuously on scrambles and offensive sweeps. As he later explained:

> The quiet desert was turned into an armada of troops, tanks and supply columns, with aircraft flying high above them also fighting in a continuous battle.
>
> I was flying Hurricanes. Our objective was to attack and stop the

The 'Ops Room' of 80 Squadron in the Western Desert, 1942.

Ju 87 Stukas from dive-bombing our troops, while keeping an eye out for any Me 109s that might be patrolling. The desert in parts seemed like a large scrap-yard with burning tanks and aircraft scattered everywhere. To me my world was real air warfare, constantly attacking aircraft and at times protecting our own.

Acting as fighter support to the advancing troops on the El Alamein front, Joe's 127 Squadron played an important part in the victory. The combat was fierce, with both sides losing many pilots. While on a patrol on 3 November, Joe very nearly fell victim to air-to-air fire. He was flying one of a group of twelve Hurricanes that encountered a formation of more than twenty-five Junkers Ju 87s and fifteen Messerschmitt Bf 109s.

Dog-fights raged all around, with Joe hitting one Stuka in the tail and another in the cockpit. In the midst of this mêlée, however, Joe's Hurricane was hit by a number of machine-gun bullets, while a cannon shell burst less than 2 feet away from him, ripping a hole in the port wing.

When Joe limped back to base he discovered that only one other Hurricane had made it back. Four aircraft had been forced to crash-land in the desert; the remainder were destroyed.

After the battle in North Africa was over 127 Squadron was transferred to Palestine, where its pilots continued to fly on convoy duties and scrambles in the eastern Mediterranean until September

Joe Willshaw DFC. (Reproduced by courtesy of Anne Kennington)

1943. By this time Joe had completed his tour of operations and had been promoted to the rank of warrant officer. He was briefly rested before being posted to 16 (Photo-Reconnaissance) Squadron, attached to the D-Day forces. This unit was equipped with Mark XI Spitfires, which were known among the pilots as 'flying petrol tanks'; they carried no weapons and their Merlin engines were specially tuned to fly in the rarefied atmosphere at 40,000 feet. Joe recalled with a chuckle: 'Apart from a camera, our only weapon was a signal flare.'

After D-Day 16 Squadron was kept busy flying reconnaissance missions to bring back vital information on enemy strengths and tank movements. Their photographs were to prove crucial in helping to coordinate ground strikes by fighter-bombers and for directing the carpet-bombing of larger troop concentrations by the 2nd Tactical Air Force. In all Joe flew sixty reconnaissance missions and was awarded the Distinguished Flying Cross in June 1945. The citation read:

> The King has been pleased to approve the award of DFC in recognition of the gallantry and devotion to duty in the execution of air operations to Pilot Officer Willshaw, RAFVR, 16 Squadron.
>
> This officer has completed two tours of operational duty. He has served both in the Mediterranean and European Theatres of War operations.
>
> In August 1944 Pilot Officer Willshaw was detailed for photo-reconnaissance of an area west of Paris. Very adverse weather, with poor visibility, was encountered over the target area, but in spite of this he started his photographic run, flying just below the cloud. Over Versailles, his aircraft was engaged by intense anti-aircraft fire and damaged. Undeterred, Pilot Officer Willshaw completed his allotted task. At all times the high standard of this officer's work has been reflected in the excellent results obtained.

Joe's gallantry medal was 'presented' to him by the postman in 1949.

'A Fine Fighting Spirit'

Maurice Smyth, a former pupil of St Leonard's School in Stafford, found employment at English Electric and worked there until early 1940 when he was old enough to enlist into the RAF and fulfill his long-held dream of becoming a fighter pilot. He qualified for his wings on 18 May 1941, and as Sergeant Smyth converted to Spitfire Mark Is. He had nothing but praise for Reginald Mitchell's creation: 'This fighter was able to out-manoeuvre any of the Luftwaffe aircraft I flew against and, despite what may be found in print elsewhere, it could even out-dive the Messerschmitt Bf 109.'

Stafford at War

On 12 August 1941 Maurice was posted to 111 Squadron at North Weald, flying Spitfire sweeps over France. He made his first sector reconnaissance two days later. On 18 August he flew on a fighter escort mission for twelve Blenheim light bombers on a raid on the Lille steelworks.

Returning from his second mission, a sweep to Hazebroke, Sergeant Smyth was 'jumped' by a number of Messerschmitt Bf 109s. He had always been told that in this sort of combat situation the best evasive tactic was to turn into the enemy. He duly followed this advice and found himself facing a pack of enemy aircraft. In the ensuing dog-fight, Maurice's Spitfire received several hits, but he managed to shoot down one of his assailants. Over the next few nights he was haunted by images of this 'trial by fire'.

Following a brief period of fruitless night-flying on interceptor patrols, Maurice was posted to 73 Squadron, then flying Hawker Hurricanes in North Africa. He arrived at Cairo on 4 July, making his first sweep over the sector four days later. The Luftwaffe had by no means been defeated in this theatre of war and on 20 July Maurice's patrol was attacked by some fifteen Messerschmitt Bf 109s, one of which sent a short burst into his Hurricane damaging the

Squadron Leader Maurice Smyth DFC, and his medal group.

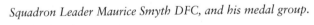

fuselage. On another occasion he was forced to make an emergency landing after running out of fuel, having chased a Junkers Ju 87 until he had it his gun-sights at a range of 300 yards.

For 73 Squadron the El Alamein offensive began in earnest on 25 October 1942, the pilots being allotted the tasks of strafing enemy columns

Squadron Leader
Smyth (left) flying a
clipped-wing Spitfire
and (below)
bombing the
Danilovgrad Bridge.

and controlling the sky over the front line. During this period Maurice had several successes, including shooting down a Junkers Ju 87 on 8 December. Further victories followed. On 15 April 1943 he destroyed a Junkers Ju 52, claiming a second damaged on the following day.

With the German army on the retreat, an isolated pocket of resistance held out around Kelibia aerodrome and 73 Squadron was sent to drop propaganda leaflets on the enemy troops in the hope of weakening their resolve. Maurice recalled how, having dropped his leaflets, he turned back across to have a look at the aerodrome, at which point the instrument panel disintegrated as anti-aircraft fire ripped through the cockpit. Maurice duly landed his damaged Hurricane back at base, unaware that he had been wounded.

Maurice's war began a new phase in July 1944 when he entered the Balkan Campaign, flying initially with 32 Squadron before joining 253 Squadron on 9 August. Both these squadrons were engaged in strafing missions in support of partisans in Yugoslavia.

Based in Italy, Maurice was to spend the next six months flying highly successful sweeps, during which he was credited with destroying 2 staff cars, more than 200 vehicles, 20 locomotives, 2 bridges, 4 barracks and a supply dump. On one particular sweep Maurice dive-bombed and destroyed an important rail bridge at Danilovgrad, thereby trapping a large German troop column as it tried to withdraw.

For his gallantry and devotion to duty Squadron Leader Smyth was awarded the Distinguished Flying Cross (*London Gazette*, 23 February 1945). The citation read:

> This officer has participated in a large number of operational sorties against mechanical transport concentrations, locomotives and land installations. On one occasion he took part in an attack against a large mechanical transport park in which 257 vehicles were destroyed or damaged. Another time, following a sortie over Dalmatia, he was forced to bale out of his aircraft and spent 16 hours in his dinghy.
>
> At all times Flight Lieutenant Smyth displayed a fine fighting spirit and pressed home his attacks with vigour and determination.

Squadron Leader Maurice Smyth DFC bombing the Danilovgrad Bridge. (Reproduced by courtesy of Anne Kennington)

Chapter Twenty

From Normandy to Germany

From as early as 1942 the Allies had been developing plans for the liberation of Europe and by late May 1944 some 800,000 fully equipped combat troops had gathered in the south of England ready to set sail in an armada of nearly 5,000 ships and landing craft.

A new programme of training began. The men of the QORR, who would be acting for the first time as close infantry support, practised disembarking from tank landing craft along the north coast of Scotland. The terrain here closely resembled that of their next battle-ground, which all knew would be somewhere in north-west Europe. By the early summer of 1944 the QORR's tanks had been brought up to full strength and supplemented with Crusaders and reconnaissance Stuarts as well as American Shermans, which made up half of their armour.

The D-Day campaign was to open up another front in Europe, while further south the Italian campaign was nearing its end. Meanwhile, in the east the Russians, who had been pushed back to the outskirts of Stalingrad, now reached a position close to their pre-war borders.

The most ideal landing-ground lay in the Pas-de-Calais, and the German commanders certainly anticipated that the Allied invasion would take place there. However, General Montgomery, working with the Supreme Allied Commander, Dwight D. Eisenhower, selected a 50-mile-long front between Caen and the base of the Cotentin Peninsula. Five beaches were chosen for the landings and were given code-names: Utah (US 4th Division); Omaha (US 1st Division and elements of the 29th); Gold (British 50th Division); Juno (Canadian 3rd Division); and Sword (British 3rd Division). On 1 June Colonel Eadie was informed of the Yeomanry's role: his men were to head the tank assault on Sword Beach, then break out from the bridgehead and take Caen.

The liberation of Europe began with airborne and commando forces destroying or securing strategic roads, bridges and gun emplacements ahead of the main landings. Meanwhile, naval and air forces began knocking out German defences in readiness for the seaborne assault.

Stafford at War

The British 3rd Division landed behind a creeping barrage laid down by
the Royal Navy on Sword Beach at 07.25 hours on D-Day, 6 June 1944.
Among those at sea awaiting the order to land were the men of the
QORR, now part of the 29th Armoured Brigade.

The tanks came ashore on the 'White' section of Sword Beach at
10.30 hours only to find themselves bogged down in a massive traffic
jam, brought about by an unusually high tide that had reduced the
expected landing area. The beach exits were heavily congested, while
the QORR's proposed assembly point turned out to be a minefield. The
plan had been for the QORR to ferry the troops of the King's Shropshire
Light Infantry (KSLI) to Caen on their tanks. However, the infantrymen
were forced to advance along the Hermanville–Beuville–Caen road on
foot, while the Yeomanry formed up ready to advance in support.

Major Tom Hassall Gardner of Rugeley, commander of the HQ
Squadron, prepared the route for the tanks. Once off the beach C
Squadron, comprising men from Burton and Uttoxeter under the
command of Major Pat B. Griffin MC, was sent to capture a ridge above
Périers-sur-le-Dan; the ridge overlooked Beuville and was a potential
source of enemy fire. Meanwhile, B Squadron, which was largely
composed of Staffordians, was to follow up and protect the right flank.
Having reached its objective, C Squadron soon came under accurate fire
and was forced to find cover. Meanwhile, A Squadron, under Major
M.A. Spencer-Nairn, was assigned to assist the men of the Suffolk
Regiment in dealing with a stronghold codenamed Hillman, which lay
further inland. The Shermans made their way along a narrow gap in the
protective minefield under cover of a five-minute artillery bombardment.
Fifty prisoners were taken following a bitter exchange of fire.

The tanks of B Squadron then came under fire as they advanced to
cover C Squadron's flank. A concealed German 88mm anti-tank gun,
which had allowed C Squadron to pass unmolested, accounted for five
tanks before it could be silenced. Lieutenant D.F. Alexander moved his
tank forward under fire to assist his troop corporal's injured crew after
their Sherman had received a direct hit. As he advanced, his own tank
was struck. Undeterred, Lieutenant Alexander ran over open ground
and dragged one man to safety, before returning to the Sherman just as
it was hit by a second shell. This gallant action was quickly followed by
another as the regiment's Medical Officer, Captain L.G. Harper, sped
forward in his half-track in an effort to rescue stranded tank crews; as
he did so, his vehicle came under fire.

The men of C Squadron were ordered to take up positions ready to
support the 2nd Battalion KSLI in clearing Beuville and neighbouring

Biéville. During the advance over exposed ground along a ridge, C Squadron was drawn into an engagement by a battery of 110mm guns concealed in woods around Périers-sur-le-Dan.

As they advanced further inland, 1 and 2 Troops of C Squadron breached an anti-tank cordon known as Pole and moved on to Lébisey, which they attacked in the early evening. Their commanding officer, Major Pat Griffin from Dunstan near Stafford, led the advance, and would subsequently be awarded a Bar to his MC for his sustained gallantry during the Normandy campaign. Meanwhile B Squadron took over the positions the C Squadron tanks had vacated to prevent an outflanking manoeuvre.

A reconnaissance by D Squadron revealed a large number of German tanks advancing from Caen, the regiment's key objective for the first day. A Squadron was ordered to move forward from its position at Hillman to engage the enemy and protect both C Squadron's rear and the earlier gains. More enemy tanks were observed making a counter-attack to the west and moving quickly for the high ground above Périers-sur-le-Dan. The tanks of B Squadron, under the command of Major G.J.W. Turner MC, had been left on Périers ridge to counter any such advance and they duly engaged the enemy.

Two Panzer IV Specials were destroyed by A Squadron, firing from their new positions to the west of Biéville, the remaining enemy armour moving into woods heading towards Le Landel. Two troops of A Squadron pursued them, sweeping over to the QORR's right flank. Meanwhile, Sergeant Joyce of 1 Troop, A Squadron, had positioned himself overlooking open ground between two woods. He saw a string of enemy tanks moving off in a line in front of his Sherman. He calmly allowed the tanks to advance into open ground before firing at the last of the column, thus preventing the rest from retreating into cover. Then he turned his 75mm gun on the four remaining enemy tanks, picking them off one after another.

More German armour advanced on the high ground above Périers, where B Squadron destroyed three and caused the remainder to pull back. The encounters had cost two Sherman tanks damaged. The wounded were evacuated to a house in Biéville, where they were cared for, under shell fire, by Mme Barrett, who was a trained nurse.

The tanks of C Squadron came under heavy shelling near the high ground at Lébisey, which overlooked both Caen and Sword Beach 6 miles to the rear. An engagement with two enemy tanks resulted in the death of Lieutenant Winterhalder, his tank and crew being driven to safety by Trooper McKinley. During the advance to the woods

Lieutenant Lionel H. Knight, 1 Troop Leader of C Squadron, earned the Military Cross; his was the furthest advance of any unit on D-Day.

As dusk descended the tanks of the QORR lay to the west of Biéville. While they had not reached their day-one objectives, they had forced back a concerted attack by the German 21st Panzer Regiment and in doing so saved Sword Beach. But it was a costly day. In the first few hours of combat the QORR lost Lieutenants D.F. Alexander and Winterhalder along with five other ranks killed, three men wounded and a further six men reported as 'missing'. Seven German Mark IVs were destroyed and two more disabled, for the loss of five Yeomanry tanks, all of which fell prey to the deadly German 88mm guns. The following days too were to see bitter combat for the men of the QORR, with inevitable losses. The battles around the town of Caen were particularly bloody.

On 27 June, as the QORR was taking part in an assault to clear woodland to the south of Chateau-de-la-Londe, the tanks came under heavy and concentrated fire. Further orders were then received, directing them first to Lébisey Wood, from where they had been forced to retreat days earlier owing to the lack of infantry support and the risk of being outflanked, and then on to Caen. The armoured breakout along the river Orne followed, with the QORR again playing their part.

With the break-up of the 27th Armoured Brigade, the QORR returned to England, where the men converted to the floating Duplex Drive (DD) amphibious Shermans. These tanks were specially adapted for traversing water, with dirigible canvas side-panels that turned them into slow-moving boats, propelled either by tracks or by a propeller. The QORR's commanding officer, Lieutenant Jim Eadie DSO, who had seen them through the trials of North Africa and the Normandy campaign, was awarded a Bar to his Distinguished Service Order and appointed as Chief Instructor at Sandhurst.

The newly promoted Lieutenant Colonel Farquhar MC led the QORR on their return to Europe, where they joined the 8th Armoured Brigade. Farquhar, a former member of the Stafford Troop, had already been awarded the Military Cross for his repeated acts of gallantry in the North Africa campaign. He had been second-in-command of the regiment when they landed on D-Day. Farquhar had six tanks destroyed under him, but each time he rallied his men, took care of the wounded and then pressed on. His gallantry earned him a Bar to his MC.

Eadie and Farquhar were not the only members of the QORR rewarded for their gallantry in the north-west Europe campaign, with both Sergeant Ken Pearce and Corporal H. Archer being awarded the Military Medal for their bravery during the Normandy operations.

The Stafford men of B Squadron were given the task of providing armoured support to the men of the 52nd (Lowland) Division during the assault on South Beveland. The DD tanks had to 'swim' 10 miles up the Scheldt Estuary before landing. Unfortunately, a combination of muddy conditions and the high banks of the dykes made it difficult for the tanks to manoeuvre, and only three reached their objective; one was that of Staffordian Jimmy Doughty, whose gallantry was rewarded with a Mention in Dispatches.

After this action the QORR was withdrawn from front-line service and re-equipped with Buffalo tanks. Now under the command of Lieutenant Colonel John Trotter, the men spent the winter training on the Maas in preparation for the crossing of the Rhine.

The Rhine crossing on the QORR's front, to the north of Rees, began at 21.00 hours on 23 March 1945, and was witnessed by Churchill and Montgomery from a nearby hill. The advance made by C Squadron, in support of the 51st (Highland) Division, was preceded by a four-hour artillery barrage. The Buffalo tanks of the QORR duly swam across the river, landing safely on the far bank; only three tanks were lost in the crossing and all their crews escaped. The remainder of the QORR landed at first light the following morning and rallied with the infantry ahead of the enemy's counter-attack.

Jimmy Doughty of the QORR was mentioned in dispatches for his gallantry during the assault on South Beveland.

The QORR later took part in the crossings of the rivers Ems and Weser, their swimming tanks leading the way and helping to gain an initial foothold on the far bank. Once ashore, the QORR dealt with any fire aimed at the vulnerable waterborne troops.

On 18 April 1945 the QORR was posted to join XII Corps in preparation for the crossing of the Elbe, which took place on 29 April. This was the QORR's last major action. During this operation Captain Thompson, Lieutenant Derbyshire and Sergeant Cass were killed, while Lieutenants Hewitt and Northcote were badly wounded. During the hard-fought campaign, Ron Daly and John Ravenscroft were both commissioned in the field, while Staffordian Frank 'The Hawk' Hawkins was awarded a CO's Commendation by Montgomery, and Major T.H. Gardner was awarded the MBE.

Les Talbot

Private Les Talbot of the King's Shropshire Light Infantry landed alongside the tanks of the QORR on D-Day. His experience of combat was to be brief, however, as he was wounded within days of landing on Sword Beach.

Len's road to war had begun with a telegram ordering him to report for military duty. Infantry training was tough by any standards, and lasted for six weeks with no rest from dawn till dusk. Initially the aim was to build up basic fitness, discipline and teamwork, and later to establish the skills of military drill and the use of rifles, grenades, machine-guns and cold steel.

Les Talbot of the King's Shropshire Light Infantry landed alongside the tanks of the QORR but was wounded not long after D-Day.

Following basic training, Les was assigned to Z Company, KSLI. As D-Day drew closer Les took part in large-scale troop manoeuvres involving landings from assault craft with close air support. All leave was cancelled and those men already away from their units were recalled. For weeks all traffic had headed southwards to temporary camps that had sprung up in semi-secrecy along the coast. Most men now knew that something big was about to happen, but no one knew exactly what or where.

On D-Day the KSLI landed as part of the 3rd Division's assault on Sword Beach. The plan was for the troops to hitch a lift on the Sherman tanks of the QORR and advance on Caen, their objective for day one. Both the British and Canadian forces quickly established wide beachheads, pushing inland until they came up against the 716th German Infantry Regiment. Caen itself was defended by a relatively small force of Germans, but stationed nearby was the crack 21st Panzer Regiment, equipped with more than 125 Mark IV Panzers and supported by 40 assault guns; once they were fully deployed in Caen the town would be a very hard nut to crack.

The 21st Panzer Regiment's tanks began to head along the main Falaise–Caen road at about 08.00 hours, little more than half an hour after the first wave of the 3rd Division's landing craft had beached. But it wouldn't be until 16.30 hours that the Panzers were in position to strike back at the invading troops.

By 11.00 hours the 185th Brigade was assembled beyond Sword Beach and ready to take that day's objective. Private Talbot's battalion had landed in good order and dispatched what little resistance they met on the beaches. Following a brief respite in an orchard near a place called Lion, they were ready to advance. The tanks of the QORR, however, were still bogged down in the congested traffic leaving Sword. An hour after their start-time the KSLI set off without tank support, which, it was hoped, would follow on.

Ahead of the KSLI lay the well-defended German position known simply as Hill 60. Initially the advance was slow, the Germans using machine-guns and small-arms fire to keep the British at bay. The Shermans of the QORR eventually caught up and were quickly able to help the infantry to press ahead and the KSLI reached the village of Biéville by late afternoon. The attack on the village descended into hand-to-hand street fighting, the men advancing house by house.

During the early stages of the battle Les Talbot had been asked to take command of his section. Les was a reluctant leader and instead opted to take charge of the Bren gun. This decision may have saved his life. While advancing through a cornfield he heard the distinctive roar of a Nebelwerfer, a six-barrelled rocket launcher. All the soldiers around him instinctively dived for cover but Les was hampered by his Bren gun and was still on his feet when the nearest rocket detonated, sending deadly red-hot splinters flying through the air. Those who had hit the deck received wounds to the head and chest, which proved fatal in one case. Les was more fortunate: the ground blast hit him in the leg. The pain of his injuries didn't register for some time and Les carried on his duties before a second blast threw him to the ground and he was eventually helped to a temporary First Aid Post. Here the wounded were assessed and later sent back to the beaches where field hospitals had already been established.

The most urgent cases were treated there and then or on-board one of the ships lying off the coast. Les was one of those who spent the evening of D-Day lying on Sword Beach as Messerschmitt Bf 109s swooped down low and strafed the men around him. He was evacuated that night. Others were not so fortunate. His CO, the medical officer and the padre were all killed in a shell hole while tending to the wounded.

The journey to Portsmouth was relatively restful, but Les was not yet out of the woods, The shrapnel that had blasted into his flesh had taken with it fabric from his clothes along with a good measure of Normandy mud. The threat of gangrene was very real and great care had to be taken with all of the casualties returning from Normandy. After spending several weeks in hospital, Les was eventually discharged, although he was unable to rejoin his regiment in action. He considered himself one of the lucky ones.

Stafford at War

The Heroes of Juno Beach

Born in Staffordshire, Bernard Blakeman has lived in the county town since before the Second World War. He served in the Royal Marines and became a member of 48 Commando, which was formed in Deal on 2 March 1944 to perform a crucial role on D-Day. Its task was to land immediately behind the western assault battalion of the 3rd Canadian Division on Juno Beach and link up with 41 Commando performing a similar role on the eastern fringes of Sword Beach with the British 3rd Division. Together these units were to bridge the gap between the two landing-grounds and prevent the enemy from mounting an encircling manoeuvre and driving a wedge between the two beaches, thus threatening the advance. The commando landing zones were not suitable for regular troops and so the much smaller marine units landed on the vulnerable sectors which they secured before pushing inland, controlling both the approaches and their flanks.

Marine Blakeman was on one of six landing craft that took 48 Commando off HMS *Warsash* ready to assault the Normandy beaches. Shells were already falling around the landing craft and Bernard recalled that within minutes two of the craft had been sunk, taking down with them 120 men. Some were picked up and rejoined the unit later in the month but many others were pulled down by the weight of their waterlogged kit and drowned.

After what seemed an age the ramps were lowered and the men hit the beach running as shells, mortar bombs and bullets impacted all around. Many of Bernard's comrades were soon killed or wounded as the German defences raked the sands with withering fire.

Members of 48 Commando training for the D-Day landings. Their role was to form a link between Juno and Sword beaches to prevent the enemy outflanking the British and Canadian troops.

COMMANDO
SERVICE CERTIFICATE

Italy	Crete	Burma	Greece
Norway	France	Sicily	Albania
Holland	Belgium	Germany	Madagascar
North Africa	Yugoslavia	Western Desert	Channel Islands

This Certificate is an Appreciation,
of Loyal Service given to Commandos by

Plyx. 105087 Mne B.Blakeman.

FEBUARY 1944.

Chief of Combined Operations

JANUARY 1946.

The Commando Service Certificate issued to Marine Bernard Blakeman.

Bernard sought cover behind one of the many anti-tank obstacles, returning fire in an attempt to suppress the enemy machine-guns for long enough to aid the general advance.

Those who got off the beach quickly headed inland for cover. Here they regrouped ready to move on their objectives. Ordered to bypass St Aubin, the marines advanced on another heavily entrenched stronghold at Langrune. Here they met stiff opposition and suffered further casualties, including a number of officers and NCOs. Meanwhile, further inland the tanks of QORR's B Squadron were preventing an outflanking manoeuvre by tanks of the 21st Panzer Regiment.

On 7 June 48 Commando captured the German strongpoint at Langrune. The fighting had been long and bitter. Since landing in the early hours of D-Day the marines had suffered 220 casualties out of their original strength of 450. Five of their six troop commanders were dead or wounded.

The commandos' next objective was the heavily defended radar station at Douvres, which they attacked on 9 June. Here they came up against members of the SS in well-entrenched positions. On 11 June the remnants of 48 Commando were sent to assist in holding the bridgehead on the east side of the Orne. Bernard and his comrades were to remain here for nearly two months, protecting the British flank and maintaining the line while the main attack was focused on Caen.

One of the vital positions 48 Commando held was Pegasus Bridge. Captured during the early hours of D-Day by glider-borne troops, the bridge was important to the Allied advance and had to be held at all costs. The commandos dug in around the wreckage of the gliders and prepared for a counter-attack. Despite being heavily outnumbered, 48 Commando went on the offensive, making raids on the German-held positions and pushing the enemy back. The Germans were so convinced that they were facing a strengthened front that they failed to take advantage of the Allies' numerical weakness.

In this battle 48 Commando fought with extraordinary bravery, both individually and as a unit. There was, however, a terrible price to pay with very many casualties, including Bernard's captain, who won the Military Cross for gallantry but did not live to learn of the award.

Stan Woodward

Perhaps one of the most remarkable Normandy stories was that of tank commander Stan Woodward. Born in Stafford on 20 April 1920, Stan Woodward attended Rickerscote School before progressing to St Leonard's. From an early age he excelled at sport, enjoying athletics and football. His real love, however, was boxing, at which he was to reign supreme at many levels and weights, during his Service days becoming Northern Command Middleweight Champion in 1941.

After leaving school Stan became an apprentice signalman, and not long after his 17th birthday he enlisted into B Troop of the QORR, with whom he was to serve in Syria and Iraq before being granted home leave in late 1940. Stan sailed on the *Empress of Britain* but missed the ship when it left dock at Cape Town, earning his passage home on another vessel by acting as a gunner. As fate would have it, the *Empress of Britain* was sunk by a German Condor long-range bomber less than 100 miles off the English coast.

Having transferred to the 3rd Royal Tank Regiment, Stan Woodward was to serve with great distinction as a tank commander during the battle for north-west Europe. His regiment was frequently in the thick of the action, particularly during operation 'Goodwood'. Here the tanks fought with close infantry support, but often found themselves spearheading an assault unaided. It was under these circumstances that Stan turned foot-soldier to great effect.

Approaching the ridge-top village of Bras the Shermans of 3 RTR found themselves facing further danger. It was here that Stan was to win the Military Medal 'for bravery in the field'. Bras was just one of many strategic villages turned into fortresses by the Germans ahead of the Allied invasion, and each village had to be fought for. Some 300 Germans defended the streets, supported by artillery and tanks. As the

Shermans pushed forward, Stan's troop-leader, Lieutenant Stubbs, was badly wounded in the head.

Lance-Sergeant Woodward immediately took control and used Stubbs' damaged tank as a barricade across the road. The narrative accompanying the recommendation for Stan's gallantry award then describes how Stan 'dismounted his crew and armed with Sten guns, revolvers and grenades, cleared the neighbouring houses and captured prisoners'. By these actions he prevented the enemy from outflanking his troop, thus maintaining the momentum of the whole attack.

Drawing of Stan Woodward. (Reproduced by courtesy of Anne Kennington)

Sergeant Woodward's crew now comprised Trooper J. Mackenzie (wireless operator); Trooper R. Stone (driver); Trooper Ashby (machine-gunner); and Trooper Dawson (gunner). They took an active part during the vital fighting around Caen and were well to the fore during the division's magnificent advance from the Seine to Antwerp, where they did good work in the dock area, taking many prisoners along the way.

Advancing across open country near Seclin, Stan's squadron once more came under fire. A troop of tanks was sent to neutralise the enemy, while the troop leader deployed Stan's Sherman to guard the main road to the south-east. He had not been in position long before he saw some Germans dash across to a wood on his right. He advanced on them and the ball-gunner, Trooper J. Ashby, blasted them out of cover with a burst of 1,000 rounds from his Browning.

Stan decided to out-manoeuvre the enemy, so went down a side-street and through a gap between some houses caught another glimpse of the Germans in their headlong flight. Ashby and Dawson finished them off while Stan searched for more Germans, picking out an 88mm gun, one of the most formidable weapons a British tank could encounter, that was covering the regiment's approach road. Dawson fired two rounds of high explosives into it as Stan selected his next target, a battery of six 88mm anti-tank guns. Their crews had just begun to load when Dawson picked them off one at a time, leaving the surviving crews to be rounded up by Belgian partisans.

As a result of this action Stan Woodward's name was put forward for a Bar to his Military Medal. The recommendation read:

This NCO, at Seclin, on 2nd September 1944, by his initiative and skill

Stan Woodward's Military Medal and Bar group. On many occasions his bravery saved his troop from suffering heavy casualties.

outflanked an enemy position of six 88mm anti-tank guns sited to hold up the advance of our troops. This NCO showed the greatest courage and determination and by crossing a stream and closing to short range he succeeded in killing or taking prisoner the entire crews of these guns. This NCO has at all times shown outstanding courage and determination to close with the enemy.

Stan's award was richly deserved: had the battery of 88mm guns been brought to bear on the Shermans of 3 RTR, there would undoubtedly have been many casualties among the tank crews.

However, Stan's acts of selfless bravery were not to end there, and he was frequently to be found leading dangerous reconnaissance patrols in order to ensure the safe advance of his troop. It was while returning from one of these patrols that Stan's luck finally ran out and he was hit in the upper leg by a sniper.

Evacuated to England, Stan was sent to Swansea Hospital. Once his wounds were healed sufficiently, however, he discharged himself and returned to his unit, eager to help prevent casualties among his men.

War News

The progress of the liberation of Europe was followed avidly via the pages of the Stafford newspapers, the *Advertiser* and the *Chronicle*. Both carried news on the general advance and more particularly details about local servicemen. Many local names were beginning to appear among the lists of dead, wounded and missing, while others would later be reported as prisoners of war. Knowledge of the plight of servicemen fighting in the local regiments helped rally those on the Home Front. The people of Stafford raised £420,192 during Salute the Soldier Week, leading up to the D-Day landings, while the grand total of monies saved, invested and donated now stood at around £4,000,000.

From Normandy to Germany

Gordon Ferneyhough

Among those who fought their way through Normandy and the Low Countries was Trooper Gordon Ferneyhough of the 2nd Welsh Guards, who served as a gunner in a Stafford-built Cromwell tank.

Ferneyhough saw action throughout the latter phases of the Normandy campaign. His battalion was assigned the particularly dangerous role of armoured reconnaissance. By early July the armoured divisions were fighting their way through the infamous *bocage*, an area of narrow lanes, thick, high hedges and overgrown embankments. It was impossible to advance on a front through such terrain, and instead combat was on a field-by-field level. Visibility was often less than 50 feet so it was ideal ambush country.

Welsh Guardsman Gordon Ferneyhough fought in a Stafford-built Cromwell tank during the Normandy campaign.

On 18 July the Welsh Guards took part in the breakout from the eastern end of the Normandy bridgehead, known as operation 'Goodwood'. This was intended to maintain the pressure in the front sector, which appeared to be flagging. In terms of men, armour and morale, however, it proved a very costly operation, the British losing 400 tanks and suffering 5,500 casualties.

The 2nd Welsh Guards' Cromwell tanks were the first to enter the Belgian capital on 3 September 1944, before advancing on to Nijmegen. Gordon's 2 Squadron was to see some of the heaviest action as the regiment made breakthrough after breakthrough, culminating in the 8-mile midnight charge along the Nordhorn–Lingen road. This advance saw the Scots Guards 'riding' the tanks in the same way they had ridden in the saddles of the Scots Greys at the battle of Waterloo 130 years earlier. Opening up the German flanks, the charge eventually led to the crossings of the Dortmund and Ems canals and the river Ems itself. Gordon Ferneyhough was present at the crossing of the Rhine at Rees, which was a major blow to the Germans. He was also with the Welsh Guards when they liberated the Westertime camp, where 8,000 British prisoners of war were discovered in various states of health. Some had been behind barbed wire for nearly five years, having been captured on the roads to Dunkirk or Calais during the retreat of the BEF.

Chapter Twenty-One

PoWs and Escapees

A number of Staffordians were captured during the war, including former King Edward VI's Grammar School pupil Leslie Gardiner.

Before the war Leslie Gardiner worked for Staffordshire County Council, where he quickly progressed and was put in charge of the county's Emergency Hospital Scheme. On the outbreak of war Leslie decided he could serve his country better elsewhere and volunteered for service with the Royal Navy. Following six months of basic training, Ordinary Seaman L. Gardiner was briefly drafted to the battleship HMS *Rodney* before being transferred to HMS *Sovereign*.

Britain, of course, relied heavily on imports and in wartime its trade routes became all the more vital. It was the Royal Navy's task to escort the large, slow-moving convoys of merchantmen in order to minimise losses through attacks by surface vessels and U-boats. For Gardiner and the rest of the crew aboard *Sovereign* this entailed shadowing merchant vessels as they sailed between Halifax in Nova Scotia and various British ports.

With a number of Atlantic crossings under his belt, Leslie was later posted to HMS *Mohawk*, a Tribal or F Class destroyer with a complement of 5 officers and 56 men. The ship's captain was Commander J.W.M. Eaton RN. At this time HMS *Mohawk* was operating in the Mediterranean, where she helped maintain the vital supply routes to North Africa, Malta and Greece. This was one of the most dangerous theatres of the war for the Royal Navy and HMS *Mohawk* was sunk on 15 April 1941. The events leading up to her loss were later recalled by Leslie:

> We arrived off Malta on the night of 10/11 April, joining the *Jervis*, *Janus* and *Nubian* as a night strike force, sailing under cover of darkness hunting German and Italian shipping and subs.
>
> The first two night patrols passed off without incident. However, on the third patrol we went searching for a convoy bound for Tripoli. Contact was made off the North African coast. Soon a fierce exchange took place. The noise was deafening. Smoke and shell-splinters filled the air. I remember our gunners worked furiously.

PoWs and Escapees

During the engagement HMS *Mohawk* was nearly rammed by the leading German merchantman, only some heroic steering by her helmsman avoiding a collision. She was, however, soon afterwards struck by a torpedo from the Italian destroyer *Tarigo*, which hit just abreast of the Y gun mounting on the starboard side:

> The whole of the stern from the superstructure aft was destroyed; she was awash as far as X mounting. The crew of the Y gun were all dead. Meanwhile the merchantman was set ablaze by A and B guns as HMS *Mohawk* lay still in the water, vulnerable to attack.

Leslie Gardiner OBE. This photograph was taken while he was still a prisoner of war.

As she wallowed helplessly, two more torpedoes struck, hitting the port side between no. 2 and no. 3 boiler rooms. The no. 3 boiler burst, scalding dozens of men as the deck ripped open.

> I joined other less badly wounded men, clambering through jagged holes blasted in the hull to reach the outside world. Within a minute *Mohawk* was listing heavily to port and soon she was on her side with no time for us to launch lifeboats. A few Carley life-floats managed to slip clear for us to scramble on to. We were two hours in the water before HMS *Nubian* picked up those who were left. There weren't many of us and most were injured or suffering from the effects of swallowing engine oil.

Leslie Gardiner pictured after the war. (Reproduced by courtesy of Anne Kennington)

The gunners of HMS *Janus* were ordered to sink the abandoned burning wreck. Forty-one of her crew went down with HMS *Mohawk*.

Following a brief period of 'survivor's leave', Able Seaman Gardiner was posted to another Tribal Class destroyer, HMS *Bedouin*, bound for duty on the Russian convoys. The appalling conditions on the Murmansk and Archangel convoys were to become legendary. Leslie recalled waves breaking

Leslie Gardiner served aboard HMS Bedouin *on the Russian convoys.*

on *Bedouin*'s deck and the salt-water freezing before it could drain back
to the ocean.

In May 1942 came a total change of scene when HMS *Bedouin* was
deployed in the Mediterranean. Sailing on one of the many convoys
that helped raise the siege of Malta, Leslie recalled the scene: 'So
intensive were the air and sea battles that all but one of the
merchantmen were sunk. During the journey we became separated
from the others and were attacked by an Italian cruiser 50 miles off
Malta.' Leslie was wounded early in the subsequent gunnery exchange.
It was standard practice to strap casualties to their stretchers while
moving them about on-board ship. Once in the vessel's sick bay Leslie
asked for the straps to be loosened. This saved his life, as when the
Bedouin sank all of the other wounded men drowned as the stretchers,
one by one, rolled over and floated away up-side-down as the ship
slipped under the waves.

Leslie spent ten hours in the water before he was rescued by the crew
of an Italian hospital ship. His trials were not yet over, though, as the
Italian doctors removed several shell splinters without the aid of
anaesthetic.

Gardiner spent a year in a prisoner-of-war camp in Genoa before
being forced into a cattle-truck bound for Austria. Among those
crammed into the same wagon were a Glaswegian and an Australian.
One had a penknife, the other part of a hacksaw blade. The three men
joined forces in a bid for freedom and after five hours' concerted effort
had made a hole in the wooden floor big enough to drop through.

The men drew lots to see who would go first. Leslie won and
prepared to make good his escape as soon as the opportunity arose:

I clambered down, hung by my fingers and toes and dropped on to the track. I bumped heavily on the sharp stones and turned my head just in time to avoid being brained by a monstrous coupling-link, swaying from side to side as it rushed past.

Leslie was able to roll off the tracks and disappear into the undergrowth unseen by the guards, and spent the next three months living off the land. Travelling only by night, he gradually made his way south towards the advancing British troops. At one point he was slightly wounded by a German motorcyclist who fired at him. He was, however, able to escape and found shelter with a family in a mountain cottage.

Having eventually linked up with the advancing British 8th Army, Leslie was sent back to England where he was granted a commission as a sub-lieutenant on a minesweeper. He was later given his own vessel, HMS *Silverton*, a Hunter Class destroyer, and retired from the Royal Navy as a commander, before spending thirty years as a travel writer and broadcaster. A regular contributor to *The Times*, the *Guardian* and the *Daily Telegraph*, he earned national recognition in his field and was awarded the OBE.

Frank Rock

Another Staffordian to be taken prisoner was Private Frank Rock, who served in North Africa and Greece with the 4th Hussars.

Mussolini had made his move on 13 September 1940 by ordering the invasion of Egypt, then under the control of the British. Frank Rock's regiment, the 4th Hussars, was among the units sent to reinforce General Wavell's army in North Africa. Here Frank served in 2 Troop, C Squadron, and was under the command of the prime minister's nephew, Randolf Churchill.

The Italians were driven back some 800 kilometres, the British putting some 130,000 men 'in the bag' and annihilating ten divisions. With victory nearly at hand, Winston Churchill moved thousands of troops, including the 4th Hussars, into Greece, which was then under threat. Meanwhile, Adolf Hitler sent German reinforcements to North Africa, pushing the British back out of all the territory they had just won. Greece too was to be invaded.

Frank recalled that the 4th Hussars had landed in Greece to a heroes' welcome, being cheered and showered with flowers by hundreds of people lining the streets. Only a few weeks later they travelled the same route in retreat. In truth, they were hopelessly out-gunned, Frank recalling that their shells simply bounced off the German tanks. As his unit fell back, Frank and a group of twenty surviving Hussars were given the task of holding a vital road leading to the Greek port of Kalavitos. Under the command of Troop Sergeant John Medley, Frank and his comrades fortified their position as best they could. As the first German tanks approached they prepared to open fire, hoping at least to knock one out with a lucky strike on the tracks. The Germans soon realised that they faced only light-calibre weapons and simply ignored them.

At the last minute, their cause lost, the order was given to try to escape. Frank was caught in the sights of a machine-gunner, the ground around him boiling with bullets. As Frank hit the deck he found a bullet hole in his tunic. Fortunately he was not wounded and managed to disappear into the undergrowth.

On the following day Frank's group of survivors was confronted by another German tank. Its commander amazed everyone with his excellent spoken English, asking them where they were going and adding the immortal words: 'For you the war is over.' The men were forced to hand over their weapons and were told to wait to be taken away by the infantry. Naturally, as soon as the tank had gone they were off. After two days on the run the men stumbled into a village where they were recaptured, joining between ten and twelve thousand prisoners of war at Kalamata. A forced march followed, during which Frank recalled being 'beaten and kicked by the guards as I lay at the side of the road, collapsed through fatigue and illness'. The march ended with the men being herded into cattle trucks bound for Austria. The train stopped briefly at Belgrade, where

Frank Rock was captured during the fall of Greece but later escaped and fought his way across Yugoslavia in the company of local partisans.

the doors slid open and the men were given black bread and water. Frank recalled: 'At the end of this four-day ordeal we arrived at Stalag 18A, where I had the best meal ever. This consisted of black bread with jam, washed down with coffee made from acorns.'

At Stalag 18A Frank saw terrible sights. The camp was divided into three sections for British, French and Russian prisoners respectively. The Russians suffered the worst:

> The Russians had a terrible time compared to us. The Germans used the excuse that they were not signatories to the Geneva Convention and therefore they could not expect more humane treatment.
>
> Typhus was often rampant in the Russian camp and they would be dying at a rate of ten to fifty a day.
>
> We often saw the Russians lining up in groups of five to receive their

daily ration of bread which they shared. There would be five men, but often three live men carried two dead between them to get the extra ration.

All of the prisoners survived on little victories over their captors. Any news from home, especially if it concerned Allied victories over the Axis Powers, was greeted with excitement and was a great boost to camp morale:

> We learned about the victories from a little radio smuggled into the camp. The Germans knew we had one and mounted surprise searches. During one of these spot-checks of the roof spaces the British PoWs stole the Germans' ladder.
>
> The most daring escape, and the one that gave us the greatest pleasure, was when a group of men stole the doctor's staff car. We watched as the guards saluted them as they passed through the gates.

Along with a number of other prisoners, Frank was moved to a work camp associated with a brickworks near Triebon. Security here was lax and Frank soon became involved in digging an escape tunnel. The Germans not only failed to notice the rise in ground level around the huts but also the fact that the soil was changing colour. Frank recalled with a smile that the tunnelling rota was even posted on the prisoners' notice-board. The tunnel was only discovered when a truck parked directly over it sank into the ground.

Meanwhile, Frank had stolen a pair of wire cutters from the factory and had smuggled them back into the camp. He used the cutters on the barbed wire and crawled through the gap to freedom. But his liberty was short-lived as he was spotted by an Austrian farmer and arrested. He was interrogated by a Gestapo officer. However, things were not as bad as they might have seemed as the officer, a former Hussar in the First World War, reprimanded Frank's police guards and sent them out to bring him a hot drink and a decent meal.

Frank was sentenced to three weeks at the Leitsen Discipline Camp, where treatment was harsh, after which he returned to Stalag 18A all the more determined to escape. The first part of his plan was to convince the commandant that his will was broken, but nothing was further from the truth.

With his risk level successfully lowered, Frank was sent to work on a farm camp at Marbourg, Yugoslavia. It was from here that he later made his escape. He had only been on the run for a few days when he came across a bridge guarded by German soldiers, who were stopping everyone and checking their papers. Having no documents, Frank would have no chance of getting across. Seizing his opportunity, he mingled in with local workers piling out of nearby factory gates and was lost in the crush.

Frank was discovered by a group of Yugoslavian partisans who at first distrusted him, as not long after he entered their camp they were attacked by a German patrol. Somehow he managed to convince them that he could be trusted and was spared. Subsequently he was to fight his way across Yugoslavia with the partisans, helping to capture a village here, destroy a German convoy there. The men moved by night to avoid enemy patrols:

> To be honest, this was just as well. The terrain was rough with hills and deep valleys. The paths were treacherous.
>
> Once the partisans had captured a town they generally celebrated. They'd commandeer all the wine and beer they could and throw a party in the hall or a barn. Things were never dull. Often they would be dancing away and a grenade or rounds of ammunition would fall from their belts. These would spin across the dance-floor.
>
> As the evenings wore on the mixture of alcohol and bravado got the better of some and when the partisans got too drunk to dance any more, then they would start drawing their guns and start picking off targets around the room, shooting at the walls and ceiling. It could get quite scary really.

Finally Frank's band of partisans reached the port of Split, which they helped to capture, assisted by a Royal Navy barrage. Frank was handed over to the crew of HMS *Birmingham*, who took him to Bari in Italy. Here he found himself denied back-pay and effectively left to fend for himself; a poor reward for his bravery and determination to get back into the war.

Things would be little different in England. Frank recalled being put on a train from Liverpool to London without even a cup of tea. Later in life Frank would reflect bitterly on the difference in his treatment by that Gestapo officer and the British authorities.

Chapter Twenty-Two

The Liberation of Europe

Although news of the Allied invasion quickly reached the civilian population of western Europe, few dared to hope that this would really be the end of their plight. Mrs Haughton (née Saint-Requir) recalled the fear that the landings might turn out to be another Dieppe and the Allies would be crushed on the beaches. However, it soon became apparent that the Americans, British and Canadians had gained a foothold and were making progress:

The Germans would always be on the move from here to there and you did not know where they would be next. They used some of the old First World War defences which no one expected and this often made things more difficult for the Allies.

People continued to disappear and hostages were executed after the invasion – if one German was killed by the Resistance then ten French men and women would be taken at random and shot. I remember one day we were led away from our house to where the Germans were selecting their victims. My mother said that she refused to stay and so defied the guns by taking us by the hand and marching us past the bewildered guards.

We lived 20 miles from the centre of Paris but my father was one of those who fought during the Battle of Paris which was part and parcel of the liberation. Although many Germans had surrendered or, fearing the mob, hid until the Allies arrived, a number of Germans and their French mistresses fought on. Throughout the battle the enemy sniped at the crowds on the street and set off booby traps.

Even when Paris had been liberated [25 August 1944] things were still not safe. When De Gaulle and the other commanders came to Paris they were shot at by the snipers; while the others bent down to take some form of cover, De Gaulle remained calm and refused to hide, showing no fear.

We formed part of the reception committee for the commanders De Gaulle, Eisenhower and Churchill, and took a gift of cigars for Churchill.

Chapter Twenty-Three

The War Against Japan

The Far East saw some of the most brutal fighting of the entire war, while still greater hardships were faced by those who had the misfortune to be taken prisoner by the Imperial Japanese forces.

Clifford Green

Clifford Green was born in Tunstall but grew up in Stafford, where he lived in one of the cottages opposite the gatehouse to Stafford Prison. Before the war he worked for Dorman Diesel at their Tixall Road site. Having been conscripted into the army, Clifford served with the West Yorkshire Regiment, the Prince of Wales's Own, as part of General Slim's 14th Army – 'The Forgotten Army' as many called it – fighting in the Burma campaign.

Both regular battalions of the West Yorkshire Regiment fought in the same theatre of war. Green served with the 1st Battalion as part of the 17th Division, which was forced to retreat some 700 miles through hostile jungle to escape the onslaught of the Japanese in early 1942. Green's battalion lost some 173 men, with a further 34 being taken prisoner; of these, only 23 lived to see the end of the war. Those who survived returned with terrible accounts of brutality.

By 1944 the tide of the war in the Far East had turned and the Japanese were on the retreat in Burma. Both battalions of the West Yorkshire Regiment played a part in the eventual defeat of the Japanese army, the 2nd Battalion as part of the 5th Indian Division.

In early February the Japanese attacked Arakan in an effort to force a way through into India. The troops of the 2nd Battalion formed a defensive box but soon found themselves surrounded by the Japanese, who occupied the higher ground and made numerous assaults, each time being forced to surrender any gained ground. The dogged determination of the 2nd Battalion was rightly praised by the Corps Commander, who wrote, 'never has any regiment counter-attacked so successfully and as often as in this battle . . . it is rare in history that one regiment can be said to have turned the scale of a whole campaign.' The failure of the Japanese to break the British line at Arakan forced them to concentrate on a new offensive to be launched further to the south, in an area held by the 1st Battalion, among other units.

Meanwhile, General Slim's plan was to form a bridgehead on the Imphal Plain. He was unaware, however, that the Japanese had already massed some 100,000 troops and were about to launch their own offensive in April 1944, in the hope that they could persuade India to throw out the British Raj. To this end the Japanese had formed two brigades of former Indian prisoners of war into the 'Indian National Army'. They knew that a neutral or pro-Japanese India would spell the end of the Allies' hopes in Burma, and so this campaign was to be given their top priority.

The Japanese advanced on the Imphal Plain with three divisions. Their targets, if achieved, would leave the surprised British cut off and without supplies. However, a Gurkha patrol sighted 2,000 Japanese on the move, while captured papers revealed that a division thought to be in the Pacific theatre had been moved to the region of Imphal. Having thus learned of the possibility of a counter-offensive, Slim decided to hold the Kohima–Imphal road. Outnumbered, his forces would be stretched to their limits, and every man who could use a weapon was sent to the front line. Here they were ordered to hold out at all costs, despite being cut off from their own lines of transport. They would be resupplied by air.

Members of the 1st Battalion who had escaped the fresh attack took up a defensive position 40 miles north-west of Imphal. Meanwhile, the 2nd Battalion, which had landed with the rest of the 5th Indian Division to the north-west of the town on 7 April, arrived at Imphal to fight alongside the 1st Battalion. Both units dug in ready for the coming battle.

The Japanese advance was met by accurate mortar and small-arms fire, and the attack, which lasted an hour and a half, collapsed without any material gains. This process was repeated again and again with fresh waves of Japanese advances. The Allies knew that they had to hold the line or the Imphal Plain would be lost. After weeks of bitter hand-to-hand fighting, the defenders of Imphal extended their control and began pushing the Japanese back along the Teddim Road.

The task of battling through towards Imphal and linking up with its defenders was given to the men of the 2nd Infantry Division. Progress against a determined enemy was slow. The siege dragged on and April gave way to May and the beginning of the monsoon season, a six-month period during which some 350 inches (30 feet) of rain falls. This made life even more difficult for the relief column and made supply drops less frequent. Disease was rife, with hundreds of soldiers suffering from typhus, malaria and dysentery.

Japanese raids on the Imphal line continued to meet with stiff opposition, although the high rate of attrition meant that the British were getting close to the point where the defences could barely be manned. However, as the siege continued the men of the West Yorkshire Regiment began to notice a difference in the attacks during June: they seemed less coordinated and more Japanese were surrendering when they were counter-attacked.

Finally the 2nd Infantry Division broke through; the two-month siege had been lifted. But the fighting was not yet over for Clifford, as both battalions of the West Yorkshire Regiment were to form part of the force that was eventually to fight its way across Burma and rout the Japanese. By November they had been pushed back as far as Kalemyo on the Chindwin river, where Clifford's regiment was finally relieved and taken out of the line for a rest. February 1945 saw both battalions of the West Yorkshire Regiment, along with the remainder of the 9th Brigade, being flown to Mektila in central Burma, miles behind the Japanese front lines. Once again they fought a determined campaign behind enemy lines, suffering heavy casualties.

Clifford Green was one of the last batch of servicemen to return to Stafford. Invalided home, he had been serving overseas since 1939, the year his daughter was born; he didn't meet her until 1946, when she was 7 years old.

Jack Maguire

Born in Eire, Jack Maguire later settled in Stafford and was for many years one of the stalwarts of the Stafford Branch of the Royal British Legion. He served with the Cambridgeshire Regiment, which formed part of the 18th Division based in Singapore. Maguire was to endure four years of hell as a prisoner of war in the hands of the Japanese. He was captured when the Japanese invaded Malaya and his unit was sent north to stop the enemy's advance:

Jack Maguire (fourth from left as a Japanese prisoner of war.

> In the jungle the enemy was often all around us. You could hear bullets hitting the ground or the men around but you couldn't see where they were coming from. We couldn't fire back because we simply didn't know where they were.

Despite their best efforts Jack and his comrades were unable to resist the Japanese onslaught and were forced into retreat. At a place called Bukit

Timah to the north of Singapore Jack came across a group of wounded British soldiers, who had been left behind and were about to be overrun. Despite the risks, he stopped to ensure they reached a makeshift dressing station where they were cared for and later evacuated.

Jack's men reached Singapore after days of travelling on foot, fighting a desperate rearguard action. Tired and running low on ammunition, they had hardly arrived when the whole garrison was ordered to surrender.

Discipline in the Japanese army was based on brutality. The officers would beat the NCOs, and they in turn beat the ordinary soldiers. To them the act of surrender was considered dishonourable. The fact that the men of the Singapore Garrison had been ordered to surrender by their commanding officers made no difference; they were forced to parade past their captors before beginning a death-march. The prisoners were treated with the utmost contempt and cruelty, as Jack witnessed for the first time not long after the forced-march began. Men, even the sick and wounded, were beaten as they tried to maintain the pace, while those who stumbled and fell were shot in cold blood where they fell.

Jack and his comrades looked on in horror, unable to act for fear of being set upon too; this inability to help haunted Jack for the rest of his life and left him with a terrible feeling of guilt. In truth he was utterly powerless and would have been shot or crucified had he laid a hand on the Japanese tormentors.

They were first marched to the prison at Changi, a place that was to become notorious. Jack remembered the brutality he witnessed here too, most disturbingly the attacks on the women from the plantations and the horrific murder of a group of Gurkhas who had been captured: 'They were bound to posts and then the Japanese took delight in the sport of bayoneting them. It was a terrible sight.'

Moved to a camp deep in the jungle, Jack was relieved to get away from the hell-hole of Changi. The jungle, however, was as much the enemy as the Japanese guards. Men caught malaria and suffered terribly from malnutrition and dysentery. Some did try to escape, but those who were caught paid the ultimate price.

Jack recalled that one group of British prisoners made it to the Burmese border before being captured. They were savagely beaten and made to walk back to the camp, their clothes tattered, their bodies covered with cuts and open sores. Their arrival was greeted by a stunned, disappointed silence, and the whole camp was forced to look on as the men expended their last efforts in digging their own graves before they were shot.

Forced to work long hours on the construction of the Burma–Siam Railway, the prisoners survived on a meagre diet of watered-down rice, with an occasional bowl of broth. It was at one of the remote work-camps that Jack and a friend decided to sneak out of the makeshift compound to trade with the locals. They were spotted while trying to get back and had to fight with a sentry who refused to accept their passive gestures of compliance.

Spared crucifixion or the bullet, they were beaten about the head with a rifle-butt by the guard they had injured, Jack losing five teeth in the brutal attack. The men were then forced into a cage where they were left crouching for days without food or water. Miraculously both men lived.

Through sheer willpower alone, Jack survived the war and was finally liberated after nearly four years as a prisoner, by which time he had lost over half of his body-weight.

Clarence Ecclestone

Staffordian AC1 Clarence Ecclestone was one of the medical orderlies whose bravery and dedication helped to save the lives of fellow prisoners working on the Burma Railway.

Clarence was evacuated by sea with other RAF personnel from Singapore a few days before it fell to the Japanese. However, his ship was attacked and eventually sank, and he was forced to swim to an uninhabited island. Later he was picked up by natives from another island who took him to Sumatra, where he was later captured by the Japanese and forced into slavery.

Clarence had served with the Stafford St John's Ambulance before the war and volunteered to act as an orderly using what he described as 'native medicines' to help those suffering from dysentery, cholera and malaria. He worked tirelessly and for a period of four months he slept for only one hour in ten. In a post-war interview Clarence recalled that the Japanese brutality knew no bounds. The prisoners were made to work up to sixteen hours a day on a starvation diet. His devoted service resulted in the award of the BEM.

Clarence Ecclestone had only a basic knowledge of first aid but was responsible for saving the lives of many sick PoWs held by the Japanese.

Chapter Twenty-Four

A Brief Period of Rejoicing

The war in Europe ended on 7 May 1945, and the next day was proclaimed 'Victory in Europe' or VE-Day. Prime Minister Winston Churchill addressed the nation by radio, broadcasting from the Cabinet Room at 10 Downing Street:

> The German war is therefore at an end . . . We may allow ourselves a brief period of rejoicing; but let us not forget for a moment the toil and efforts that lie ahead. Japan, with all her treachery and greed, remains unsubdued.

VE-Day celebrations in Stafford's Pitt Street, May 1945.

A number of street parties were held in and around the town, these being repeated to a lesser extent to mark the victory over the Japanese a few months later. However, because the celebrations had become somewhat random, and as returning servicemen had largely missed out on the festivities, it was decided to put a halt to the disorder and arrange a VE-3 Day, which was designated as 24 September 1945.

The nation came together again to celebrate the hard-won peace on 8 May 1946, with a Victory Parade held in London. Among those selected to take part were Cyril Green of 14 Battalion (Stafford) Home Guard, Major Kenneth Pearce MM of the QORR, Corporal Reginald Smith of the RAF Regiment, and Wing Commander R.G. Fisher of the RAF. High above the crowds Warrant Officer W. Edwards and Flying Officer Alan Wilson flew in the Lancaster bombers that took part in the celebratory fly-past.

Stafford's Comforts Fund had been redesignated the Welcome Home Fund on 9 December 1944. With the 'bank' standing in the region of £4,000, over a quarter of it was spent during Welcome Home Week, returning soldiers being invited to a celebratory banquet on 6 June 1946. The remainder of the fund was used to assist servicemen and women who experienced financial hardships.

On 15 June 1946 Stafford granted its highest honour, the freedom of the borough, to the men of the North and South Staffordshire Regiments, the QORR and 241st Super-Heavyweight Battery (Stafford Battery) RA.

In June 1946 the North Staffordshire Regiment, the South Staffordshire Regiment, the Staffordshire Yeomanry (QORR) and the Stafford Battery were all granted the Freedom of Stafford.

Chapter Twenty-Five

RAF Establishments

By 1941 the need to train new pilots and air crews to take the air campaign to the enemy required additional Operational Training Units (OTUs), Landing Grounds (LGs) and other Air Ministry establishments. This led to work beginning on a number of new sites, including a number close to Stafford.

Hixon

RAF Hixon lay 4 miles to the north-east of Stafford. Its three runways were 1,650, 1,400 and 1,200 yards long but were restricted by the North Staffordshire Railway and the LNER's Stafford–Uttoxeter line.

Construction work began during the summer of 1941 and the airfield was handed over to 93 Group on 11 May 1942, becoming a satellite station of RAF Lichfield, with 30 OTU being formed here on 28 June 1942. Towards the end of their training airmen were posted to various OTUs to form up for the first time as crews before transferring to Heavy Conversion Units and then on to operational squadrons.

Hixon's first aircraft, Wellington ICs, were ferried in from 12 OTU on 15 July 1942 and by early August the unit had accepted its first intake of thirty air crew. Their training began with take-offs and landings, known as 'circuits and bumps', followed by more complicated trips including cross-country navigational exercises, practice bombing and fighter affiliation exercises.

The bombing range, to the west of Sherbrook Valley on Cannock Chase, was less than 5 miles from Hixon. The target itself was a roundel of bright white-glazed ceramic shards with a painted yellow central brick obelisk. It was not always successfully hit and night flares or smoke-bombs often fell several miles away. A second range used by 30 OTU was at Bagot's Park.

Part of the flying programme included dropping propaganda leaflets over northern France. Such sorties were known as 'Nickel' raids and they sometimes attracted the attention of anti-aircraft fire and enemy night-fighters, occasionally resulting in the loss of aircraft.

Sometimes the 30 OTU crews also flew diversionary attacks, known as 'Bullseye' missions, designed to draw the Luftwaffe's night-fighters away from Bomber Command's main raids. Such missions might involve a number of OTU aircraft flying towards the enemy coast before altering course and returning to base. The OTU crews also flew on operational missions, joining aircraft from regular squadrons, particularly on 'Bomber' Harris's 1,000-Bomber Raids.

Air crews based at Hixon took part in their first bomber mission on the night of 13/14 September 1942, on a raid to Bremen. Two days later the target was Essen. Both raids cost Bomber Command dearly, but the locally based air crews were luckier than most, escaping without casualties.

On 16 September 1942 Hixon acquired a satellite station at Seighford, which often remained open when Hixon was forced to close due to worsening weather conditions.

Hixon's first fatal air accident occurred during a night-bombing exercise on 31 October 1942. Vickers Wellington Z1083 was making its landing approach when the pilot, believing he was going to overshoot the short runway, decided to pull up and go round again. But the Wellington had lost too much airspeed and stalled at 500 feet, crashing at Grange Farm, Amerton, with the loss of all her crew.

In January 1943 30 OTU began receiving Wellington Mark IIIs along with their ground crews from the soon-to-be-disbanded 25 OTU based at Finningley, Yorkshire. Mark X Wellingtons were to arrive later, with Hixon's surplus bombers being ferried to RAF Seighford.

The first of Hixon's Wellington IIIs to crash was lost with all her air crew on 7 February, coming down close to the Old Rectory at Ingestre Park. Once again the cause was a stall while the pilot was trying to go round for a second attempt at landing. Another Wellington crashed near Hasting Wicket, 2 miles to the east of the airfield, while returning from a night-navigation exercise on the night of 6/7 July.

On 10 September an RAAF crew was lost while landing. The accident followed the usual pattern, with the pilot trying to pull up to go round again. This time the Wellington III cleared the perimeter fence but struck a house, killing all of her crew.

Wellington III BK179 crashed at Ranton Woods less than five minutes after taking off from Hixon airfield on 10 April 1943. Another local crash occurred on 10 February the following year when a Wellington X came down in a field close to the airfield. The wreckage quickly caught fire. All the crew clambered to safety apart from the unfortunate navigator, Sergeant A.J. Welstead, whose parachute harness became tangled in the wreckage, leaving him suspended over the flames.

On this occasion local baker Cyril Fradley was awarded the British Empire Medal for his courageous attempts to save Welstead. Another local air crash occurred on 8 January 1945 when a Wellington X, piloted by Flight Sergeant L.J. Porter, crashed at Burton Lane, Eccleshall. There were no survivors.

In July 1943 single-seater fighters came on to the scene at Hixon when 1686 Bomber (Defence) Training Flight arrived with its American-built Curtiss P-40 Tomahawks. These aircraft, which acted as 30 OTU's Fighter Affiliation Unit until it was disbanded on 21 August 1944, still bore the distinctive shark's teeth nose art used on their operational squadron, 112 (Shark) Squadron.

A notable VIP visit came when General Patton passed through RAF Hixon briefly on 30 June 1944, while on his way to the prisoner-of-war camp at Rugeley.

In early 1945 30 OTU left RAF Hixon, being replaced in February by 12 (Pilot) Advanced Flying Unit ((P) AFU), which was eventually equipped with over fifty Blenheim Is, IVs and Vs, with a number of Bristol Beauforts arriving in May. The unit was disbanded in June 1945, when RAF Hixon became a storage facility for RAF Stafford.

Seighford

Work began at RAF Seighford in June 1941. The station, 4 miles to the west of Stafford, became operational on 16 September 1942, when it was handed over to 30 OTU, Hixon. Initially Seighford was equipped with Vickers Wellington ICs, but in December 1943 the first Mark IIIs arrived, followed by Mark Xs. The main runway at Seighford was able to accommodate Avro Lancasters, some of which flew out of the airfield from May 1943, although the Wellington remained the unit's mainstay.

All OTUs suffered casualties and RAF Seighford was no exception, with losses due to weather conditions, poor maintenance, metal fatigue, incorrect installation of parts, and, of course, pilot error. In all, ninety aircraft were damaged beyond repair. The cost in terms of human life was even greater, with nearly 200 fatalities in four years of wartime flying.

Lost or damaged bombers from operational units based elsewhere occasionally took advantage of Seighford's long runway when other suitable airfields were closed due to bad weather. On one occasion a B17 of the USAAF made a forced landing there with wounded crew aboard following a daylight mission over Germany; both the pilot and second pilot were carried out on stretchers.

There were those who didn't quite make it, too. One bomber came down near Thornyfields Lane, possibly while trying to make an approach on the runway. Another fatality was ferry pilot Captain Perrin, USAAF, who crashed at Creswell on 4 July 1944. Perrin was heading north in his damaged P-51 Mustang, flying parallel with the Eccleshall Road, when leaking fuel exploded. He may have sighted the airstrip at Seighford earlier and then tried to make for it but his Mustang crashed several miles short, just beyond Stafford's Holmecroft housing estate. Today a plaque marking the crash-site records how Perrin stayed at the controls long enough to steer the stricken aircraft away from local houses.

Captain Perrin had become a fighter ace prior to serving as a ferry pilot, as illustrated by the swastikas painted on the fuselage of his fighter aircraft.

On 28 October 1944 the 23rd Heavy Glider Conversion Unit arrived, RAF Seighford becoming a part of Training Command and acting as a satellite for RAF Peplow in Shropshire.

From early November that year Seighford became home to twin-engined Armstrong Whitworth Albemarle II and VIs, used to tow the troop-carrying Airspeed Horsa I and II gliders, along with the CG-A4 Wacos, American heavy gliders known by the RAF as the Waco Hadrian I. The crossing of the Rhine was set for early 1945 and ahead of this critical date training was intensified, with consequent losses among both the Albemarle and glider crews. Seighford was also the site of mock combat landings, while glider assault troops 'fought' the Home Guard in the nearby woods during their battle training.

RAF Establishments

It was in mid-November, part-way through the glider training programme, that RAF Seighford saw another invasion, this time of American B17s. On 16 November American bases across East Anglia had dispatched their aircraft bound for a daylight raid on Aachen. Fog closed in during the day and only Seighford remained open and operational. A total of thirty B17s landed that afternoon; a further twenty-five were forced to divert and landed at Seighford the next day, parking up alongside the other aircraft. The air crews were temporarily quartered at the American Depot at Stone, there being no places available at nearby Seighford Hall, which was used as a YWCA hostel for off-duty WAAFs from the station.

It was during this period that Joe Willshaw dropped in, having experienced 'engine trouble'. Willshaw landed his photo-reconnaissance Spitfire during one of his non-operational flights, handing it over to the station's engineers for them to give the engine an overhaul. Meanwhile, Joe's younger brother was waiting for him at the gates with a spare bicycle and the two made the short journey to Doxey, where the family enjoyed a rare Sunday lunch together. It was an amicable arrangement; the 'erks' got to work on a Spitfire and Joe, who was not long back from serving in North Africa, spent a little time with his delighted family.

In January 1945 RAF Seighford became a satellite of 21 ((P) AFU) Wheaton Aston, former home base of Battle of Britain veteran Ernest 'Gil' Gilbert. Wheaton Aston had opened in 1941 and was the parent station of RAF Perton and RAF Tattenhall (from January 1944). Pilots trained under the Empire Training Scheme received a refresher course and additional night-flying training on Airspeed Oxfords at Wheaton Aston before being posted to an OTU.

As the Allies overran Poland and Germany they liberated a number of prisoner-of-war camps. Over the following weeks hundreds of repatriation missions were flown by converted Lancaster bombers, each carrying up twenty-five former prisoners. RAF Seighford and Hixon were among the airbases handling the mass repatriation, the former receiving nearly a thousand men a day.

Not all repatriations had a happy ending. Staffordian Private William Arnold of the RAOC, captured in France during June 1940, survived nearly five years at Ludwigslut only to perish in an air accident on his way home.

The Advanced Flying Unit's work continued, although at a reduced pace from the mid-summer of 1945, until 21 ((P)AFU) and the RAF left Seighford in early December 1946. Both Seighford and Wheaton Aston were converted into temporary accommodation for displaced Polish service personnel. Among those billeted at Wheaton Aston was the former SOE agent Zdzislaw Luszowicz, who later made Stafford his home.

Stafford

Stafford's 16 Maintenance Unit was opened on 1 December 1939. Built near Beacon Hill, it lay close to the site of an airstrip developed in 1916 for one of the many Home Defence Squadrons established as a countermeasure against the growing Zeppelin menace. The Stafford airstrip was suitable for Tiger Moths and Magisters, and was used for transportation and communication purposes. When the Secretary of State for Air, Sir Archibald Sinclair, visited 16 MU on 3 May 1944, however, he landed at nearby Hixon and made the journey to RAF Stafford by staff car.

Following the cessation of hostilities, RAF Stafford received surplus parts from all over the country and from liberated Europe, and the site became one of the RAF's (and later NATO's) main Maintenance Units.

The Fauld

To the east of Stafford were the disused gypsum mines in the area known as the Fauld. It was here that 21 MU, a massive underground bomb store, was located. At 11.11 hours on 27 November 1944 disaster struck when a huge explosion rocked the Fauld. The blast was so great that it was felt all across the county. Sixty-one people died, and it left a crater three-quarters of a mile across and more than 400 feet deep. It was the largest man-made explosion before the atom bomb and was recorded on seismographs as far away as Casablanca. Fire crews from Stafford attended the scene but there was little that could be done. Any remaining stable munitions were removed from the labyrinth of tunnels and transferred to Tattenhall, which became the RAF School of Explosives.

Penkridge

RAF Penkridge, 6 miles to the south of Stafford, was a Remote Landing Ground, first used by 29 EFTS in September 1941 but soon adopted by 28 EFTS. Meanwhile, a dummy factory was constructed at Brewood to divert the Luftwaffe from the Boulton Paul factory 6 miles away.

Chapter Twenty-Six

Gallantry Awards

Key:
LG = *London Gazette*
SC = *Stafford Chronicle*

Sergeant Robert Francis Wyness RAF
LG 17/5/40   Distinguished Flying Medal
The award to Sergeant Wyness was related to that of Squadron Leader Miles Villiers Delap (05149), whose citation read:

> During March 1940 this officer was the pilot of an aircraft engaged in a reconnaissance flight over the Heligoland Bight. Whilst penetrating into a strongly defended area, as he descended through cloud to about 1,000 feet a submarine was sighted moving slowly on the surface. Squadron Leader Delap immediately attacked from about 500 feet allowing the submarine no time in which to submerge. He released a salvo of four bombs and two direct hits were observed.
>
> Squadron Leader Delap then continued the reconnaissance which produced valuable results.

Wyness lived in Stafford after the war.

Flying Officer R. Wyness DFC, DFM (far right) and Squadron Leader Hughie Edwards VC DFC (second from left). Wyness was a navigation officer with 105 Squadron and planned the route for the Bremen Raid during which Edwards was to earn his Victoria Cross.

Sergeant John Downing RA
LG 11/7/40   Distinguished Conduct Medal
The recommendation for this award read:

> Sergeant Downing displayed great gallantry in maintaining the service of a gun of which he was No. 1, during the 1st and 2nd June 1940 at Dunkirk dockyard, whilst under heavy shell fire and low-flying bombing attacks of the enemy. He put up a very effective fire which dispersed several low-flying attacks on the Mole and undoubtedly saved it from severe damage.

Sister Nellie Goodwin, Territorial Army Nursing Service
LG 27/9/40   Order of the British Empire (Military)
'For distinguished services rendered in action in connection with recent operations in Norway.'

Acting Flight Lieutenant Charles Maxwell Owen RAFVR (210 Squadron)
LG 10/11/40   Distinguished Flying Cross
The recommendation for this award read:

> This officer worked extremely hard and with exceptional keenness as convoy escort. His long record of meeting and escorting convoys successfully far out in the north west approaches would be difficult to excel. Latterly he has been engaged on long and very dangerous flights in very bad weather. Throughout his operational career, Owen has displayed exceptional keenness and unflagging devotion to duty.

Chief Officer Harry Grattidge of Cunard White Star Ltd, Liverpool
LG 4/10/40   Order of the British Empire (Civil)
Part of the general citation for gallantry awards connected to the sinking of the SS *Lancastria* read:

> The SS *Lancastria* had embarked a large number of troops and some refugees at St Nazaire, and was waiting for her escort when attacked. She was struck by a salvo of four high explosive bombs, which hit her simultaneously in the most vital parts, and she sank in ten minutes. Some 2,000 were saved by life belts and 500 by boats and rafts.

It is estimated that the *Lancastria* was carrying 5–6,000 souls when she rolled over and sank. The loss constituted the worst disaster at sea during the entire conflict.

Flying Officer Donald Wilfred Steventon RAF
LG 31/10/41   Distinguished Flying Cross

Gallantry Awards

Sergeant Denis Norman Smith RAFVR (144 Squadron)
LG 21/11/41   Distinguished Flying Cross

Lieutenant James Malcolm Stuart Poole RN (HM Submarine *Urge*)
LG 28/11/41   Distinguished Service Cross

Lieutenant Patrick John Morgan RN (HMS *Penelope*)
LG 20/2/42   Distinguished Service Cross

Lieutenant John Stuart Comery RA
LG 10/7/42   Military Cross
'In recognition of gallantry and distinguished service at Malta.'

Lieutenant James Malcolm Stuart Poole DSC, RN (HM Submarine *Urge*)
LG 29/9/42   Bar to Distinguished Service Cross
'For bravery and devotion to duty on successful submarine patrols in HMS *Urge*.'

Flight Sergeant Alec William Blakeman RAFVR
LG 1/1/43   Mention in Dispatches

George Horatio Nelson, Director of English Electric Co.
LG 1/1/43   Knighthood

Major (Acting Colonel) G.F. Haszard OBE, DSC, RN
LG 1/1/43   Commander of the British Empire (Military)

Pilot Officer John Maguire RAFVR (158 Squadron)
LG 14/1/43   Distinguished Flying Cross
'As air gunner, Pilot Officer Maguire has participated in very many sorties and has proved himself to be a most reliable member of aircraft crew. He has displayed great skill and vigilance and his coolness and resolution in the face of enemy fire have set an excellent example.'

Squadron Leader Donald Wilfred Steventon DFC, RAF (541 Squadron)
LG 5/2/43   Distinguished Service Order

Sergeant Horace John Roe RAF (500 Squadron)
LG 16/2/43   Distinguished Flying Medal
Joint citation with the award of a Distinguished Service Order to Acting Squadron Leader Michael Anthony Ensor DFC, RNZAF, of the same squadron. The citation read:

In November 1942 Squadron Leader Ensor and Sergeant Roe were captain and rear gunner of an aircraft employed on an anti-submarine patrol. During the flight a U-boat was observed on the surface of the sea and Squadron Leader Ensor attacked it from a height of 50 feet, causing it to blow up. The force of the explosion caused severe damage to the aircraft. Sergeant Roe, after reporting the damage to his captain, left his turret and with complete disregard for his own safety, commenced jettisoning all movable equipment in an effort to assist his captain to keep the aircraft airborne. Squadron Leader Ensor made great efforts to retain control but, although he succeeded in climbing to 1,500 feet, one engine failed and he was compelled to give orders for the aircraft to be abandoned. In the face of most harassing circumstances Squadron Leader Ensor, gallantly supported by Sergeant Roe, displayed courage and devotion to duty of a high order.

Squadron Leader George Hassall Nelson-Edwards RAFVR (93 Squadron)
LG 26/2/43   Distinguished Flying Cross
The recommendation for this award read:

This officer's devotion to duty and sheer hard work have contributed largely to the successes gained by his squadron. He has destroyed at least three enemy aircraft. In addition his fine leadership during several low-level machine-gun attacks has enabled highly successful results to be achieved.

Flight Sergeant John Arthur Bott RAF (83 Squadron)
LG 12/3/43   Distinguished Flying Medal

Engine Room Artificer Third Class John Foster Hart RN
LG 6/4/43   Mention in Dispatches

Acting Squadron Leader Geoffrey Wilson O'Neill Fisher DFC, RAF
LG 14/5/43   British Empire Medal (Military)

Captain John Hilary Dorman RAMC
LG 1/6/43   Military Cross
Awarded 'in recognition of gallant and distinguished service in the Middle East'.

Lieutenant Colonel George Richard Samuel Fisher, CO 14 Battalion (Stafford) Home Guard
LG 2/6/43   Order of the British Empire (Military)

Gallantry Awards

Mr William Martin Rowland, Joint Managing Director, Universal Grinding Company Ltd
LG 4/6/43   Member of the British Empire (Civilian)

Acting Squadron Leader Geoffrey Wilson O'Neill Fisher OBE, DFC, RAF (101 Squadron)
LG 11/6/43   Bar to the Distinguished Flying Cross
The recommendation read:

> He has displayed outstanding leadership and ability and pressed home his attacks with the utmost determination, often in the face of intense opposition. In February, by his prompt action and fearlessness, he extricated a crew from a burning aircraft, though he knew the petrol tanks were likely to explode at any moment. In the air, his missions (including sorties against such heavily-defended targets as Hamburg, Cologne and Berlin, and Tripoli and Benghazi) have invariably been completed with outstanding coolness and determination.

Acting Flight Lieutenant James Scott Walker RAFVR (46 Squadron)
LG 11/6/43   Distinguished Flying Cross

Lieutenant Sidney Charles Jervis RE
LG 24/6/43   Mention in Dispatches
'For gallant and distinguished service in the Middle East during the Germans' stay in Alamein.'

Sergeant Bernard Augustine Gottwaltz RAF (49 Squadron)
LG 20/7/43   Distinguished Flying Medal

> One night in June 1943, this airman was the flight engineer of an aircraft [Lancaster] which attacked Cologne. Whilst over the target area, the bomber was hit by anti-aircraft fire. The starboard outer engine caught alight but Sergeant Gottwaltz dealt with the situation promptly and effectively. Some time later the port inner engine became faulty but Sergeant Gottwaltz was able to keep it functioning until his pilot [Wing Commander Johnson] reached an airfield in this country. Throughout the return journey, this airman displayed great skill and devotion to duty, contributing materially to the safe return of the aircraft.

Squadron Leader Donald Wilfred Steventon DSO, DFC, RAF (541 Squadron)
LG 20/7/43   Air Medal (USA)
This award was conferred by the President of the United States of America.

Captain (Temporary Major) David Morris RHA
LG 22/7/43   Military Cross
'In recognition of gallantry and devotion to duty in North Africa.'

Leading Telegraphist Joseph Robert Stockton RN
LG 27/7/43   Distinguished Service Medal
The recommendation read: 'For daring enterprise and skill in successful patrols in HM Submarine in the Mediterranean.'

Sergeant Kenneth Flavis Winter RAF (78 Squadron)
LG 17/8/43   Distinguished Flying Medal
Awarded for 'gallantry and devotion to duty in air operations'.

Lance-Bombardier Kenneth Hone RA
LG 19/8/43   Military Medal
Hone wrote a letter home explaining how, during the Battle of Gabes Gap, he went out and rescued his major, who was wounded and lying in open ground which was being heavily shelled. Hone reached the officer and tended to his wounds before dragging him 50 yards to a place of relative safety, collecting four other wounded men en-route.

Pilot Officer Eric Arthur Johnson RAFVR (472 (RCAF) Squadron)
LG 14/9/43   Distinguished Flying Cross

Trooper John William Sillitto, QORR, RAC [attached to the SAS]
LG 14/10/43   Military Medal
'For service in North Africa.'

LG 21/10/43   Bar to the Military Medal
'For service in Sicily.'

Flight Lieutenant David Henry Blomeley RAF (605 Squadron)
LG 22/10/43   Distinguished Flying Cross
The citation read:

> This officer has undertaken a very large number of sorties and his efforts have featured great skill and resolution. One night in August 1943, following a successful attack on an enemy airfield, he engaged an enemy fighter and shot it down. In operations since then, Flight Lieutenant Blomeley has destroyed 2 Junkers 88s. His excellent record is worthy of high praise.

Gallantry Awards

Sergeant John William Sillitto served with the Staffordshire Yeomanry before joining the Special Forces. After gaining his parachute wings, he served with the Long Range Desert Group in North Africa and later fought in Sicily, earning the Military Medal and Bar. He is seen here with his proud parents outside the gates of Buckingham Palace following the award ceremony.

Sergeant Harold Cork RAFVR (77 Squadron)
LG 16/11/43   Distinguished Flying Medal
Awarded for 'gallantry and devotion to duty in the execution of air operations'. The citation read:

> His navigation [during 300 hours of operations against the enemy] has been of a consistently high standard, and his determination and efficiency have been largely responsible for his crew's success.

Sergeant F.P. Griffiths RASC
LG 13/1/44   Mention in Dispatches
'For service in North Africa.'

Sergeant F.P. Griffiths of the Royal Army Service Corps.

Pilot Officer Alec William Blakeman RAFVR (83 Squadron)
LG 18/1/44   Distinguished Flying Cross

Acting Squadron Leader Richard Jack Fursman RAF (413 (RCAF) Squadron)
LG 7/3/44   Distinguished Flying Cross

Petty Officer Motor Mechanic David George Welton RN
LG 30/5/44   Distinguished Service Medal
'For outstanding courage, leadership and skill in light coastal craft in many daring attacks on enemy shipping in enemy waters.'

Cyril Fradley, Baker and Confectioner, Hixon, Staffordshire
LG 40/5/44   British Empire Medal (Civil)
Probably the only such award to a baker in the whole of the war, part of the recommendation for Fradley's medal read:

> When an aircraft crashed and caught fire three members of the crew jumped to safety just as the flames were spreading from the port engine to the pilot's cabin. The fourth member of the crew was caught by his parachute harness as he was climbing out of the cabin and was left suspended on the side of the burning fuselage.
>
> Fradley, and others, ran forward to release the airman but they were driven back by the intense heat. Fradley, however, made a second attempt. Undeterred by the flames and exploding ammunition, he returned to the blazing wreckage, grasped the airman round the legs and lifted him clear. Unfortunately, the airman died some hours later from his injuries.
>
> Fradley was severely burned about the face and hands when making his gallant attempt to save a life.

Pilot Officer Harry Gilbert Nixon RAFVR (166 Squadron)
LG 2/6/44   Distinguished Flying Cross

Flight Lieutenant Denis Norman Smith DFM, RAFVR (109 Squadron)
LG 8/6/44   Mention in Dispatches

Flight Lieutenant Frank Leslie Dodd, RAFVR
LG 8/6/44   Air Force Cross

Major John Thomas Harper, Canadian Infantry Corps
LG 8/6/44   Member of the British Empire (Military)

Flying Officer A.W. Blakeman RAF
LG 18/7/44   Distinguished Flying Cross

Flight Lieutenant Frank Dodd AFC, RAF (544 Squadron)
LG 2/8/44   Distinguished Flying Cross

Trooper Daniel Francis Draper RAC (4/7th Royal Dragoon Guards)
LG 31/8/44   Military Medal
'In recognition of gallant and distinguished services in Normandy.'

Trooper Daniel Francis Draper of the 4/7th Royal Dragoon Guards, RAC, was awarded the Military Medal for gallantly saving the lives of another tank crew trapped in their burning Sherman.

Flight Lieutenant Frank Dodd flew with various photo-reconnaissance units. He discovered the Tirpitz moored in Altafjord on 12 July 1944. (Reproduced by courtesy of Anne Kennington)

Flight Lieutenant James Cotton Martin Mountford RAF
LG 1/9/44   Distinguished Flying Cross

Flight Lieutenant Frank Dodd AFC, RAF (544 Squadron)
LG 8/9/44   Distinguished Service Order
Dodd was later awarded a bar to his AFC and made a Commander of the British Empire. He remained in the RAF after the war and attained the rank of Air Vice-Marshal.

Flying Officer George Herbert Dennis RAFVR (218 Squadron)
LG 8/9/44   Distinguished Flying Cross
The recommendation read:

Flying Officer Dennis has taken part in many sorties, a large number of which have been against strongly defended targets in Germany. He is a navigator of high merit and his excellent work has contributed materially to the success achieved. His example of keenness and devotion to duty has been worthy of great praise.

Flying Officer George Herbert Dennis of 218 Squadron RAFVR was awarded the Distinguished Flying Cross 'for courage and devotion to duty under very hazardous conditions'.

Flight Sergeant Roger James Bowen RAFVR (97 Squadron)
LG 15/9/44   Distinguished Flying Medal
The recommendation read:

> This airman has completed, in various capacities, many
> successful operations, in which he has displayed high skill,
> fortitude and devotion to duty.

**Acting Wing Commander Donald Wilfred Steventon DSO,
DFC, RAF (544 Squadron)**
LG 3/10/44   Bar to the Distinguished Flying Cross
His citation read:

*Flight Sergeant
Roger Bowen
RAFVR.*

> This officer is in command of the squadron to which many missions have
> been assigned since the invasion of northern France. In the planning and
> execution of these operations, Wing Commander Steventon has
> displayed outstanding skill and tactical ability and much of the success
> achieved can be attributed to his sterling work. On two occasions Wing
> Commander Steventon successfully completed sorties which demanded
> the highest standard of skill and courage. The photographs which he
> secured were a splendid testimony to his outstanding efforts.

Lance-Sergeant Frederick Benjamin Bradshaw RE
LG 19/10/44   Military Medal
This medal was awarded 'in recognition of gallant and distinguished
service in north-west Europe'. The recommendation read:

> Sergeant Bradshaw was in command of a section of sappers landing with
> an assault company of infantry at Le Hamel on 6 June 1944. Their task
> was to make crossings over ditches for mortars and heavy weapons. Two
> of his five men were knocked out, but Sergeant Bradshaw continued
> under heavy fire and laid all the light bridges. He then returned to the
> beach and organised a gapping party under shell-fire. His display of
> courage was outstanding.

Pilot Officer Stanley Martin Hicks RAFVR (10 Squadron)
LG 17/10/44   Distinguished Flying Cross

Pilot Officer Walter Hutchinson RAF
LG 4/11/44   Distinguished Flying Cross

Captain Norman Leslie Hamilton (Yorkshire & Lancashire Regiment)
LG 14/11/44   Military Cross
'For gallantry in Italy.'

Gallantry Awards

Lance-Sergeant Stanley Clifford Woodward RAC (3 RTR)
LG 21/12/44   Military Medal
'For gallantry in north-west Europe.'

Sergeant Kenneth John Pearce RAC (QORR)
LG 21/12/44   Military Medal
'For gallantry in north-west Europe'. The recommendation read:

> On 8 July 1944 Sergeant Pearce was acting as a troop leader in the assault echelon during the attack on Lébisey. He gave most excellent support to the infantry, and dealt effectively with enemy machine-guns which were holding up their advance. He was then ordered to proceed to the high ground south of Lébisey. His troop located two dug-in enemy tanks and by very skilful manoeuvring he enabled his troop to destroy both of them without loss. His wireless operator was then wounded, but in spite of heavy fire from enemy artillery, mortars and anti-tank guns, he pushed on to his objective. From there he engaged many targets and passed back most excellent information, until at last his tank was hit by an anti-personnel shell and he was forced to pull back. He showed great drive and determination, with complete disregard for his own safety, and his actions had a large bearing on the successful outcome of the operation.

Corporal Stanley Clifford Woodward MM, RAC (3 RTR)
LG 1/3/45   Bar to the Military Medal
'In recognition of gallant and distinguished service in north-west Europe.'

Major (Temporary) George William Haggis RE
LG 11/1/45   Mention in Dispatches
'In recognition of gallant and distinguished service in Italy.'

Ordnance Mechanic Aubrey Marsden RN
LG 30/1/45   Distinguished Service Medal
Marsden's award came as part of a series, under a general heading announcing two Distinguished Service Medals and nine Mentions in Dispatches: 'For courage, leadership and skill in HM ships *Bellona*, *Kent*, *Myngs* and *Verulam*, in the destruction of an enemy convoy off the coast of Norway.'

Flight Sergeant Thomas Edwin Drew RAFVR (156 Squadron)
LG 16/2/45   Distinguished Flying Medal
Drew was an air gunner who had flown sixty operations prior to his award.

Flight Lieutenant Maurice William Smyth RAFVR (253 Squadron)
LG 23/2/45 Distinguished Flying Cross

Lieutenant Peter William Hodgens RA
LG 8/3/45   Military Cross
This was awarded in recognition of Hodgens' 'gallant and distinguished service' in Italy. The recommendation read:

> Lieutenant P.W. Hodgens was the forward observing officer with C Company. After the capture of the position, heavy artillery and mortar fire was brought down by the enemy but Lieutenant Hodgens continued to register and control the supporting artillery with the greatest coolness and disregard for danger.

Sergeant Trevor Myatt RAF (582 Squadron)
LG 13/3/45   Distinguished Flying Medal
The citation read:

> Flying Officer Thorby, Flight Sergeant Carroll and Sergeant Myatt were navigator, wireless operator and mid-upper gunner respectively in an aircraft piloted by Flying Officer McVerry in an attack on the oil refinery at Zeitz one night in January 1945. Although two engines became troublesome soon after leaving base, Flying Officer McVerry used them most skilfully and was able to reach the target on time. During the bombing run the aircraft was hit by fire from the ground defences whilst illuminated in the searchlights. Nevertheless Flying Officer McVerry held to a steady run until the bombs were released. Shortly afterwards the aircraft was attacked by a fighter. Serious damage was sustained. The elevator controls were rendered useless and the bomber went into a steep dive. Flying Officer McVerry succeeded in levelling out but for the remainder of the flight he was faced with the greatest difficulty in retaining even a measure of control. The position was most alarming but with great coolness Flying Officer Thorby worked out a new course and the aircraft headed towards Allied territory. Meantime, Flight Sergeant Carroll and Sergeant Myatt had gone to the assistance of the rear gunner who lay wounded and trapped in his gun turret. In total darkness and lacking oxygen, all but one of the supply bottles having been broken, they worked heroically. Although badly hindered by the manoeuvres of the aircraft, which was constantly diving and climbing, they succeeded in freeing their comrade. At this point Flight Sergeant Carroll collapsed. He revived, however, after being given oxygen by Flying Officer Thorby, who had carried him forward. When Allied territory was reached, Flying Officer McVerry gave the order to abandon the aircraft. Before jumping

themselves, these crew members prepared their injured comrade for the parachute descent and released him first. Afterwards all came down safely. In circumstances of great peril these members of the aircraft crew displayed the highest standard of bravery, coolness and resolution.

All of those mentioned were awarded the Distinguished Flying Cross or the Distinguished Flying Medal. Despite their efforts to save him, the rear gunner was discovered dead in the snow.

Pilot Officer Arthur Herbert Smith RAFVR (236 Squadron)
LG 20/3/45   Distinguished Flying Cross

Sergeant W.M. Cains RA
LG 22/3/45   Mention in Dispatches
'In recognition of gallant and distinguished service in north-west Europe.'

Lieutenant Colonel William James McIntosh RAMC
LG 31/3/45   Order of the British Empire (Military)
'For services in north-west Europe.'

Corporal (Acting) John Wyatt (Wiltshire Regiment (Duke of Edinburgh's))
LG 12/4/45   Military Medal
After the war Wyatt lived in Stafford.

Lieutenant Colonel (Temporary) William Vernon Harry Robins (2/The King's Royal Rifle Corps)
LG 26/4/45   Distinguished Service Order
'In recognition of gallantry and devotion to duty in Italy.'

Flight Lieutenant Basil Henry Francis Templer RAFVR (540 Squadron)
LG 8/5/45   Distinguished Flying Cross

Police Constable William Poole, Staffordshire Constabulary
LG 8/5/45   British Empire Medal (Civil)

An aircraft crashed in a field and burst into flames. Poole ran to the scene of the crash and through a hole in the fuselage he could see the rear gunner who was unable to release himself. The constable dropped his greatcoat and tried to get the man out but the hole was not big enough and the heat drove him off. He then picked up his greatcoat and, holding it between himself and the flames as protection, returned to the machine. This time he succeeded in getting the gunner out and dragged him clear. Poole showed courage and devotion to duty without regard for his own safety.

Sergeant (Acting) Arthur Montague Thomas Heritage (Grenadier Guards)
LG 10/5/45   Military Medal
'In recognition of gallant conduct and distinguished service in north-west Europe.'

Pilot Officer (bomb-aimer) Vernon Thomas Marshall Wilkes RAF (150 Squadron)
LG 25/5/45   Distinguished Flying Cross
The recommendation read: 'For displaying utmost fortitude, courage and devotion to duty in numerous operations against the enemy.'

Pilot Officer William Joseph Willshaw RAFVR (16 Squadron)
LG 1/6/45   Distinguished Flying Cross

Acting Flight Lieutenant John Arthur Bott DFM, RAF (158 Squadron)
LG 14/6/45   Mention in Dispatches
Bott lived in Stafford after the war.

Mr Robert Stribley Murt, M.Inst.CE, County Surveyor, Staffordshire
LG 15/6/45   Order of the British Empire (Civil)
'For services to Civil Defence'.

Lady Dorothy Meynell JP, President, Staffordshire Branch, British Red Cross Society
LG 15/6/45   Order of the British Empire (Civil)

Major (Temporary) George William Haggis RE
LG 28/6/45   Member of the British Empire (Military)
Haggis was serving with the 8th Army in October and November 1944, and this award was made in recognition of his 'gallant and distinguished service in Italy'.

Gallantry Awards

Captain (Temporary) Geoffrey Frederick Senior RA
LG 5/7/45 Military Cross
'In recognition of gallant and distinguished service in Italy.'

Temporary Acting Leading Seaman Frederick Morgan MN
LG 10/7/45 The Netherlands Bronze Cross
This cross was presented by Her Majesty Queen Wilhelmina of Holland for Morgan's gallant service as a gun-layer on the Dutch motor vessel *Franz Hals* on 2 November 1942. He remained at his post throughout a lengthy dual with an enemy U-boat, during which nine torpedoes were launched at his vessel, several exploding within close proximity. During the engagement he demonstrated 'courage and determination by maintaining accurate fire under dangerous circumstances'.

Temporary Acting Leading Seaman Frederick Morgan was awarded the Bronze Cross for his gallant service.

Lieutenant John Nigel Risley Hearn (Grenadier Guards)
LG 12/7/45 Military Cross
'In recognition of gallant and distinguished service in north-west Europe.'

Acting Squadron Leader James Scott Walker RAFVR (128 Squadron)
LG 17/7/45 Bar to his Distinguished Flying Cross
Walker flew 81 operations, 31 as captain of a Lancaster and 50 on Mosquito bombers. His recommendation read:

> Since the award of the DFC, this officer has shown keen interest and determination throughout his operational tour, and has achieved great success.

Acting Squadron Leader James Scott Walker of 128 Squadron RAFVR was awarded the Distinguished Flying Cross and Bar.

Lance-Sergeant John Thomas Sammons, Royal Signals
LG 2/8/45 British Empire Medal (Military)
'In recognition of gallant and conspicuous conduct in north-west Europe.'

Corporal Maynard Aubrey Cotton RAC (1st Derbyshire Yeomanry)
LG 23/8/45 Military Medal

Lance-Bombardier V.T. Hooper RA
LG 29/11/45   Mention in Dispatches
'In recognition of his gallant and distinguished service in Italy.'

Lieutenant-Colonel   Guy   Johnson   German (Leicestershire Regiment)
LG 11/10/45   Distinguished Service Order
'In recognition of gallant conduct and distinguished service in the field, Norway Operations, 1940.'

Flight Lieutenant Denis Norman Smith DFM, RAFVR (109 Squadron)
LG 4/12/45   Distinguished Flying Cross
The recommendation read:

Lance-Bombardier V.T. Hooper of the Royal Artillery.

> This officer has completed two tours of operational duty. His outstanding ability and unfailing determination to complete his allotted tasks have been an asset to his squadron. He has participated in numerous sorties, many of which have been against the heavily defended Ruhr area. At all times Flight Lieutenant Smith has displayed a high standard of devotion to duty.

Flying Officer Malcolm Albert Peterson RAF (692 Squadron)
LG 7/12/45   Distinguished Flying Cross

Warrant-Officer Class I Raymond Kilford REME
LG 13/12/45   Member of the British Empire (Military)
'For service in the Italy campaign.'

Sergeant George Arthur Robotham RAF
LG 1/1/46   British Empire Medal
This award is believed to have been made for Robotham's gallantry in rescuing crashed air crews in Italy.

Mr J.H. Wears
LG 12/1/46   Order of the British Empire (Civil)

Sister Edith May Rawes, Territorial Army Nursing Service
LG 17/1/46 Royal Red Cross 2nd Class

Sergeant George Robotham won the British Empire Medal in Italy in early 1945.

Gallantry Awards

The recommendation for Sister Rawes' service in Burma read:

> During this period when the unit was working at very high pressure and under adverse conditions, the standard of care and attention that the casualties received in the Nursing Officer's ward was of a very high standard. Her enthusiasm and devotion to duty, her tireless and unselfish attention to the wounded, was magnificent.

Warrant Officer Claude Adams served with the 4th KSLI. His Distinguished Conduct Medal was announced in 1946 and may have been for gallantry in Normandy where his unit served.

Captain George William Riley RA
LG 24/1/46   Member of the British Empire (Military)
'For service in north-west Europe.'

Warrant Officer Class II (Acting) Claude William Adams, 4/KSLI
LG 24/1/46   Distinguished Conduct Medal
'For service in north-west Europe.'

Sergeant G.E. Tagg RA (formerly of the Stafford Battery)
LG 23/5/46   Mention in Dispatches

Vice-Admiral Charles Eric Morgan CB, DSO
LG 13/6/46   Knight Commander of the Bath

Captain (Temporary) Stanley Frederick Knight RE
LG 13/7/46   Member of the British Empire (Military)
This award was made for service as a bomb disposal officer.

Acting Wing Commander Donald Wilfred Steventon DSO, DFC, RAF
LG 26/7/46   Croix de Guerre 1940 with Palm (Belgium)

Sergeant G.E. Tagg, formerly of the Stafford Battery, was mentioned in dispatches.

Lieutenant Colonel G.J. German DSO (Leicestershire Regiment)
LG 1/8/46   Mention in Dispatches
For service in Norway or Colditz.

Aircraftman Class I Clarence Ecclestone RAFVR
LG 1/10/46   British Empire Medal (Military)

'In recognition of gallant and distinguished service rendered whilst a prisoner of war in Japanese hands.'

Zdzislaw Luszowicz
1947   The King's Medal for Courage in the Cause of Freedom.
Luszowicz lived in Stafford after the war.

Wing Commander Donald Wilfred Steventon DSO, DFC, RAF
LG 17/10/50   Distinguished Flying Cross (USA)
This award was conferred by the President of the United States in recognition of services rendered during the war period 1939–45.

The following were awarded Montgomery Certificates for gallantry and devotion to duty in north-west Europe:
SC 28/4/45   **Sergeant S.J. Davis RE (148 Field Park Squadron)**
SC 5/5/45   **Private N.H.P. Davies (Wiltshire Regiment)**
SC 16/6/45   **Bombardier S.T. Chilton RA (Stafford Battery)**

Exhaustive searches of the *London Gazette* have thus far failed to produce the gazette dates of the following awards that were announced in the local press:

SC 3/1/41   Mr A Walsh: Member of the British Empire (Civil)
SC Jan 1942   Flight Lieutenant George Hassall Nelson-Edwards: Mention in Dispatches
SC 30/5/42   Flight Lieutenant J.C. Robinson RAF: Distinguished Flying Cross
SC July 1943   Eric Gosling: Mention in Dispatches
SC 1/7/44   Driver C. Robertson, 14 Company RASC: Mention in Dispatches
                 'For gallantry in Lybia on 2 June 1944.'
SC 4/45   R. Binns, Royal Scottish Fusiliers: Mention in Dispatches
                 'For service in Burma.'
SC 7/10/44   Sergeant F.R. Perks, Reconnaissance Corps: Mention in Dispatches
                 'For gallantry in France in spotting enemy mortar positions and troop concentrations.'
SC 21/10/44   Flight Lieutenant George James Mountford: Air Force Cross
                 'For devotion to duty during 2,000 hours of operational flying in the mid-Atlantic in anti-U-boat warfare.'

Gallantry Awards

SC 25/11/44   Captain N.L. Hamilton, Yorkshire and Lancashire Regiment: Military Cross

SC 16/1/45   Flying Officer Henry Britton: Distinguished Flying Cross
Awarded for 35 operations over north-west Europe.

SC 21/7/45   Lance-Corporal Robert Brown, 14th Army, Burma: Mention in Dispatches

Lance-Corporal Robert Brown served with the 14th Army in Burma and was mentioned in dispatches for his service in the Far East.

SC 10/8/46   Captain Walter Dean RA: Mention in Dispatches
'For gallant and distinguished service in north-west Europe.'

SC 14/12/46   Major C.E. Woolcock: Mention in Dispatches
'For distinguished and gallant service in the Mediterranean Theatre.'

Major C.E. Woolcock was mentioned in dispatches for his 'distinguished and gallant service in the Mediterranean Theatre.'

SC 1946   Craftsman R. Williams REME: Commendation for brave conduct.

SC 1946   Lieutenant Commander H.B. Hinks RN: Distinguished Service Cross
'For service in the Far East.'

SC 1/1/44   Stoker Petty Officer George William Wetton RN: Distinguished Service Medal

'For gallantry and outstanding service in the face of the enemy and upholding the fine traditions of the Royal Navy.'

SC 1/1/44   Flight Lieutenant D. Page: Distinguished Flying Cross

SC 29/8/44   Flying Officer Dennis RAF: Distinguished Flying Cross

Possible candidates for this award are:

1. Pilot Officer Edward John Dennis RAFVR (104 Squadron): *LG* 3/3/44

2. Acting Flight Lieutenant William Richard Dennis RAF (158 Squadron): *LG* 68/12/44

On 8 September 1945 Winston Churchill was made a Freeman of the Borough of Stafford.

Chapter Twenty-Seven

Casualties of War

The people of Stafford served with great distinction on the Home Front and in every theatre of the war. In all some 180 Staffordians were to be killed during nearly six years of death and destruction before Nazi Germany, Fascist Italy and the Japanese under Emperor Hirohito were defeated.

The names of many of Stafford's war heroes were inscribed in a Book of Remembrance now held in St Mary's Church, which is regularly opened on a different page to allow the names to be read by visitors. Each name represents a story, most of them as yet untold.

Those who lived in the Weeping Cross area are remembered on the Weeping Cross memorial. Various private memorials and plaques were commissioned by local employers, including Lotus Shoes, the ICI Salt Works and English Electric. Churches also produced memorial rolls and plaques, including the former St Alban's Church. The King Edward VI's Grammar School Memorial survives and was transferred to the Highfields site when the school moved.

Key:
* = Not in St Mary's Remembrance Book
DoW = Died of Wounds
EE = English Electric Memorial
KE = King Edward VI's Grammar School Memorial
KIA = Killed in Action
LP = Lotus Plaque
S&DPO = Stafford & District Post Office Memorial
SGI = Died in Stafford General Infirmary
WX = Weeping Cross Memorial

(Name, service number, rank, unit and details of death and memorials)
ACFORD, Leslie Charles, 4921861, L/Cpl, 185th Provost Coy, Corps of Military Police. KIA Antwerp 16/12/44.

ANDREWS, Robert George, LP.

ARNOLD, William Ernest, 5046876, Pte, 7th Ordnance Stores Coy, RAOC. Taken prisoner at Dunkirk; killed in air crash while being repatriated on 25/4/45.

ASH, Clarence, 4917906, Pte, 2nd Airborne Bn, South Staffs. Regt. KIA Arnhem, 25/9/44.

ASHLEY, Robert George, P/JX173851, Able/S, HMS *Hood*. KIA Atlantic, 24/5/41.

ASKEY, George Albert, 1909744, L/Sgt, Bomb Disposal Section, RE. KIA Greece, 3/7/45.

BADGER, Reginald George, 2819722, WO II CSM, 156th Bn, Parachute Regt, AAC. KIA Arnhem Pocket, 18/9/44. WO Badger was awarded the Montgomery Certificate in May 1944.

Reginald George Badger served in the 156th Parachute Regiment and was killed in the Arnhem Pocket on 18 September 1944.

BAILEY, Frank, 755977, Dvr, 1st Reserve Motor Transport Coy, RASC. KIA Alamein, 11/6/42.

BAILEY, Ronald, 2738652, Gdsm, 3rd Bn, Welsh Guards. KIA 4th Battle of Monte Cassino, 27/5/44*.

BAKER, Cyril, P/JX5117096, Ord/S, HMS *Lagan*. KIA on Atlantic convoy, 20/9/43. Buried at sea.

Staffordian Cyril Baker served on the frigate HMS Lagan and was killed in action on 20 September 1943.

BASHFORTH, Alan Peyman, 1578122, Sgt, RAFVR. Died Wales, 8/2/44.

BASSETT, Harold Frank, 7936725, Tpr, 6th Royal Tank Regt, RAC. KIA Gothic Line, 9/9/44.

Harold Frank Bassett served with the 6th Royal Tank Regiment and was killed during the advance on the Gothic Line on 9 September 1944.

BATES, Frank, 4917909, Pte, 2nd Airborne Bn, South Staffs. Regt. KIA Nijmegen, 19/9/44.

BEECHING, Kenneth Roy, 156654, Capt. Attached 6th Bn, Royal Inniskilling Fusiliers. KIA Tunisia, 3/4/43.

BEESON, John Edward, 143764, Lt, 60th Field Regt, RA. Died South Africa, 7/7/42, KE.

BETTERIDGE, Cyril Percival, 2617103, Gdsm, 3rd Bn, Grenadier Guards. DoW Gothic Line 9/10/44*.

Guardsman Cyril Percival Betteridge was serving with the 3rd Grenadier Guards when he died of wounds received during the assault on the Gothic Line.

Sergeant Reginald Claude Betts flew Halifax Bombers with 102 Squadron. He was killed on the Magdeburg Raid on 22 January 1944.

BETTS, Albert C/SSX29116, Able/S, HM Submarine *Utmost*. KIA Mediterranean, 25/11/42.

BETTS, Reginald Claude, 1618081, Sgt, 102 Sqn RAFVR. KIA Magdeburg Raid, 22/1/44.

BLOOR, Brian Cotter, 76255, Fl/Lt, 916 (Balloon) Sqn RAFVR. Died UK, 28/8/41*.

BOON, Ernest Moreton, 1233069, WO Obsv. 211 Sqn RAFVR. KIA Burma, 28/5/44, KE.

BOON, John, 40597, PO, 150 Sqn RAF. KIA Douzy Bridge Raid, 14/5/40. KE*. Buried in Douzy Communal Cemetery, Ardennes, France.

BOOTH, Cyril Norman, 4927447, Fus. 6th Bn, Royal Scots Fusiliers. KIA Normandy, 8/8/44.

Cyril Norman Booth of the 6th Royal Scots Fusiliers pictured here as a sergeant in the local Army Cadets. Booth was killed in action in Normandy on 8 August 1944.

BOYDON, William Bernard, 5255098, Pte, 7th Bn, Worcestershire Regt. Died 3/11/41. Buried in Stafford Cemetery, Staffordshire (New Portion 58).

BRADBURY, Gordon Stephenson, 7448093, Sgt, 44 Sqn RAFVR. Died UK, 6/8/44.

BROUGH, Edward, 14259976, L/Cpl, 2nd Airborne Bn, South Staffs. Regt. DoW Arnhem, 19/9/44.

BROWN, Horace Thomas, 14417202, Pte, 5th Bn, Dorset Regt. KIA Arnhem, 17/9/44.

Horace Thomas Brown of the 5th Dorset Regiment was killed at Arnhem on 17 September 1944. He worked for the English Electric Company and was a member of the Corporation Street Boys' Choir.

BROWN, William Donald, 945000, WO A/G, 7 Sqn RAFVR. KIA Berlin Raid, 20/1/44, KE.

BUCKETT, Ernest Gordon, 4857293, L/Cpl, 1st Bn, Leicestershire Regt. KIA Malaysia, 3/1/42.

BUTLER, Robert, 139687, FO/Bomb Aimer, 97 Sqn RAFVR. KIA Berlin Raid, 16/12/43, KE.

Robert Butler, a former pupil of King Edward VI Grammar School, was killed in action during a raid on Berlin on 16 December 1943.

BURNE, Roger Sambrooke, 756741, Capt, 244th Battery, 61st Field Regt, RA. KIA Normandy, 3/8/44.

CARLESS, Donald James, 14577949, Gnr, 9th Bn, Middlesex Regt. Died of illness, Belgium, 2/11/44, EE.

Donald James Carless served with the 9th Middlesex Regiment and died in Belgium on 2 November 1944. He too had worked for the English Electric Company.

CARTWRIGHT, George William, CH/X3213, Mne, HM Landing Craft Gun 16, RN. Killed on Landing Craft, St Ann's Head, 26/4/43.

CARTWRIGHT, William Eric, 14402359, Pte, 2nd/5th Bn, The Queen's Royal Regiment. KIA Italy, 9/9/44.

CHESTER, Harold James, 964552, F/Sgt, 228 Sqn RAFVR. KIA 12/6/44, KE.

Casualties of War

CLARKE, Albert, 940903, Sgt, 75 Sqn RAFVR. KIA Germany, 28/9/43, LP.

CLARKE, Harry Kitchener, 4037521, Cpl, 4th Bn, King's Shropshire Light Infantry. Belgium, 4/9/44, St Paul's Plaque.

CLARKE, John Raymond, Able/S, RN. KIA during air raid on Sicily, 29/8/43*.

CLAY, Charles Henry, 5348635, Tpr, 147th (10th Bn, Hampshire Regt) Regt, RAC. Died Germany, 4/5/45.

CLAY, Oswald Charles, 557368, Tpr, Staffordshire Yeomanry. KIA Normandy, 8/6/44.

CLEWS, Cyril, 5953824, Pte, 5th Bedfordshire & Hertfordshire Regt. Died as a PoW in Burma, 29/6/43.

CLOUSON, Stanley, 504820, Cpl, North Somerset Yeomanry. KIA Damascus, 10/7/41.

CONCAR, Bernard Patrick, 14654763, Pte, 6th Bn, North Staffs. Regt. DoW Normandy, 9/7/44.

CONNOLLY, Patrick John, D/LX611991, Ldng-Stwd, HMS *Minster*. KIA Normandy operations, 8/6/44.

Patrick John Connolly, a leading steward on HMS Minster, *was killed on 8 June 1944 during the Normandy operations.*

COOPER, Edward Roy, 2221308, Sgt A/G, 75 (New Zealand) Sqn. DoW Germany, 28/12/44.

Sergeant/Air Gunner Edward Roy Cooper of 75 (New Zealand) Squadron died on 28 December 1944 from wounds received when his Lancaster bomber was shot down over Germany.

COOPER, Ronald David, 14418605, Pte, 2nd Bn, Border Regt. Died India, 5/6/44, EE.

CRUTCHLEY, Norman Stanley, 4924918, Pte, 2nd (Airborne) Bn, South Staffs. Regt. KIA 4th Battle of Cassino, 9/7/44.

DAVIS, Ronald Charles, 4110560, L/Sgt WOp, The Queen's Bays (2nd Dragoons), RAC. DoW Egypt, 3/6/42.

DAY, Francis, 4127744, Pte, Cheshire Regt. Drowned, Birkenhead Docks, 10/1/40, EE, KE.

DAY, Geoffrey Walter, C/JX639876, Able/S, HMS *Aldenham*. KIA Adriatic, 14/12/44, EE.

DEAKIN, George Edward, 14771916, Pte, South Staffs., June 1944/3rd Bn, Monmouthshire Regt. KIA Netherlands, 2/4/45.

George Edward Deakin was killed in action while serving with the South Staffordshire Regiment in the Netherlands on 2 April 1945.

DEWHURST, Vernon Bramwell, 61506, PO, RAFVR. Flying accident, 2/5/41, KE.

DINGLEY, Albert Henry, 1166735, Sgt/Pilot, RAFVR. KIA Egypt, 4/6/42.

DODD, Joseph Bentley, 1579089, Gnr, 503rd Battery, 79th Searchlight Regt, RA. Died UK, 1/4/43, St Alban's Plaque.

DORMAN, Stephen Littlewood BA (Camb.), 100249, Major, RE. KIA Tunisia, 18/12/42.

DOWNING, George Henry Gerald, 14409625, L/Cpl, enlisted in Royal Warwickshire Regiment aged 17; served in 8th Bn, Parachute Regt. DoW Germany, 28/12/42.

DRURY, William Horsman, 1178920, F/Sgt Pilot, RAF. Died UK, 1/9/42, KE.

EASTWOOD, Leslie Moorhouse, Second Radio Officer, SS *Holmside* (Newcastle-on-Tyne), Merchant Navy. KIA 19/7/41 KE*, Tower Hill Memorial.

ECCLESTONE, G.T.J. ('Bert' on St Alban's Plaque), 1479435, Dvr, Royal Corps of Signals. KIA Libya, 6/9/41. St Alban's Plaque.

EDKINS, Henry Jackson, Cpl. KIA, *c.* 21/4/45.

ELEY, Frederick Eric, 145829 FO, 619 Sqn RAF. KIA Konigsberg Raid, 30/8/44.

EVERETT, John Huskisson, 894422, Gnr, Pre-war Territorial RA. Later 67 Field Regiment, RA. KIA 21/04/43, Medjez-El-Bab War Cemetery 12.E.5.

FALLOWS, George, Sub/Lt, HMS *Jackdaw*, FAA. Died 12/12/44, Lee-on-Solent, FAA, Memorial, Hampshire.

FELLOWS, Henry, Sgt RA. Formerly a member of the Stafford Battery. DoW after a shell accident in India, 10/8/45.

Casualties of War

FLATTERS, K. Apprentice, MV *Jedmoor* (London), Merchant Navy. KIA 16/9/41, KE. Tower Hill Memorial, London, UK Panel 59.

FLETCHER, Leonard Victor, 1273972, AC2, 23 Sqn, RAF. Flying accident, 21/6/41, St Alban's Plaque.

FLINT, Dick, 5046188, Sgt, North Staffs. Regt. Died 16/1/40.

FLINT, Edgar Joseph, 6914217, Rfmn, 2nd Bn, Rifle Brigade. KIA Alamein, 27/10/42.

FOLLOWS, Frederick William, Sub-Lt/Pilot, HMS *Furious*, RN, FAA. Killed in aircraft accident, Gibraltar, 1/7/41, KE.

FOLLOWS, Henry Harry, 8449056, Sgt, 8th Field Regt, RA. Died India, 10/8/45.

FOLLOWS, William Oliver, 5260221, Pte, 6th Bn, Green Howards (Yorkshire Regt). Died Tunisia, 9/4/43.

FRYER, Albert (G. on VM), 14407958, Sgt, 8th Bn, Parachute Regt, AAC. KIA Normandy, 6/6/44.

GARLEY, Albert Victor, 7518544, Sgt. KIA Cassino, 15/5/44, LP*.

GAULT, Basil Thomas, 2623833, Sgt, 1st Wing, Glider Pilot Regt. KIA Arnhem, 20/9/44.

GILLEN, Eamonn, 2221440, Sgt, 100 Sqn, RAFVR. KIA Hanover Raid, 5/1/45.

GLOVER, George Edward, 10600668, L/Sgt 1st Regt, Reconnaissance Corps, RAC. KIA Tunisia, 3/5/43.

GLOVER, Harold Arthur, 937635, AC1, RAFVR. SGI, on leave, 28/12/41, EE.

GLOVER, Jeffrey, 1169260, Sgt/Pilot, 102 Sqn RAFVR. KIA, shot down by night-fighter off Dutch coast on Kiel Raid, 1/11/41.

GORE, Samuel George, 14401191, Pte, 1st Bn, Wiltshire Regt. Died 20/2/44 EE. Buried in Taukkyan War Cemetery.

GRAHAM, Eric Leslie, Lt, HMS *Quebec* RNR. Died off Boulogne, 19/9/42, KE*.

GREY, Stephen Charles, 7253737, Pte RAMC. Burma Railway, 8/1/43. Buried in Chungkai War Cemetery, Thailand (12.E.7).

GROUCOTT, Stanley Joseph, 1581803, Sgt FE, 434 (Royal Canadian Air Force), Sqn. KIA Berlin Raid, 29/1/44, WX*.

HACKETT, Bernard Laurence, T/152827, Dvr, 903 Motor Brigade Group Coy, RASC. KIA Salerno Bridgehead, 18/9/42*.

HACKETT, John F., T/152828, Dvr, No. 1 Support Group Coy, RASC. KIA El Alamein, 14/11/42.

HAGGETT, Harry, 626994, Sgt A/G, 51 Sqn RAF. KIA, lost during raid on German power station, 17/8/40.

HARPER, John Thomas MBE, Major, North Staffs. in First World War; Instructor, Cadet College, Canadian Forces, in Second World War. Died UK, November, 1944.

HARRISS, John E.*

HASSAL, Alfred, 1033548, Dvr, 59th Medium Regt, RA; attached 235 Battery. Killed in a road accident in the Netherlands during an offensive, 13/2/45.

HAWKINS, Francis George, T/871363, Dvr, RASC. Died UK, 2/7/40, EE.

HAWKINS, Joshua, 4918760, Bdr, 61st Heavy Regt RA. KIA Italy, 25/11/44, LP*.

HEALEY, Joseph Michael, 1582388, Sgt A/G, 103 Sqn RAFVR. KIA on Cassel Raid, 22/10/43, EE.

HEENAN, John Andrew, 1583786, Sgt Nav. 70 Sqn RAF. Crashed in southern Italy on supply drop to Yugoslavia, 29/12/44.

HENN, Douglas Owen, 324803, Sgt, Staffordshire Yeomanry. Normandy, 18/7/44*.

HEWARDINE, Walter Leonard Peatfield, Surg. Lt, HMS *Tumult*, RN. KIA UK, 21/6/43, KE.

HIGGINBOTHAM, Brian, 742629, WO Pilot; after 22 months' operational flying, he was posted to No. 6 OTU, Coastal Command RAFVR. Killed in air accident while instructing night-flying, 1/10/42, EE.

HILL, Alfred James, CSM, North Staffs Home Guard. Killed in grenade accident saving the lives of his comrades, 11/11/42.

HILL, Harold Roy, 157975, Sgt, 514 Sqn RAF. KIA Nuremberg raid 31/3/44, EE.

HITCHEN, John Thomas, 157742, PO, 83 Sqn RAFVR. KIA Berlin raid, 3/1/44, EE.

HODGSON, J.H., KE*.

HODSON, Alfred Arthur Henry (A.H.H. on VM), 819663, Sgt, A/G, 576 Sqn RAFVR. His Lancaster was attacked by a Ju 88 during a night raid on Mailly la Camp, 4/5/44.

HOLDEN, Kenneth John, 14766586, Tpr, 44th Royal Tank Regt. Died Germany, 14/4/45.

HOLMES, Douglas John, Temp. Lt, Royal Marine Group. KIA during the defence of Crete, 22/5/41.

Casualties of War

HOLT, Stanley John, 755357, Sgt, WOp/A/G, 99 Sqn RAFVR. His Wellington was shot down into the sea by a Ju 88c off the east coast of England while on Mannheim Raid, 30/4/41.

Stanley John Holt served with 99 Squadron as a wireless operator/air gunner flying Wellington bombers.

HOPKINSON, Edward Vincent, 938242, Sgt Air Observer, 55 Sqn RAFVR, (Middle East Command). KIA Egypt, 22/2/42 LP*.

HORNE, ??, Royal Fusiliers. Died after sustaining a dog bite in Greece, 8/3/45.

HOWARTH, John, LP*.

HUNTER, Leonard Cyril, 105312, Major, 2nd Bn, Sherwood Foresters (Notts. and Derby. Regt). KIA Anzio, 4/2/44 KE*.

JACKSON, Martin Edward, 4033082, L/Sgt North Staffs Regt. DoW after a grenade accident, 27/4/44.

JAMES, Kenneth, 1096410, Gn, 51 Field Battery RA. KIA Alamein, 23/12/41.

JAMES, Ronald, Sgt, WOp, A/G. KIA 28/12/41.

JEPHCOTE, Frederick, 5125147, Pte, 1st Bn, East Kent Regt. KIA Cassino, 31/5/44*.

JOHNSON, Harry, 172880, PO, 578 Sqn RAFVR. KIA on Karlsruhe Raid, 24/4/44, EE, WX.

JOHNSON, James, 176437, FO, RAFVR. KIA on Walchen coastal gun battery raid, Flushing, 21/10/44.

JOHNSON, John Francis, 4341810, Sgt, 2nd Bn, East Yorkshire Regt. DoW Sword Beach, D-Day, 6/6/44, S&DPO*.

JONES, Harry Offland, 7044035, L/Cpl, 1st Bn, Royal Irish Fusiliers. KIA Cassino, 3/11/43

JONES, Herbert Leonard Price, 2360997, Cpl, Royal Corps of Signals. KIA Cassino, 4/4/44, EE.

JONES, William John, 5047726, Cpl, 2nd Bn, West Riding Regt. KIA Burma, 23/2/42.

JUPP, Anthony Dallas, Midshipman/Observer, HMS *Peewit*, RNVR. Killed in a flying accident in Angus, 29/8/44, EE.

KENT, John, LP*.

Stafford at War

KENWOOD, Norman, C/JX351294, Able/S, HMLCA, 591. KIA in the D-Day Landings, 6/6/44, LP*.

KEMP, Oscar Compton, C/JX130904, PO, HMS *Dasher*, RN. Died 27/3/43 KE*. Chatham Naval Memorial, Kent, UK 68.1.

KESSON, Edward, 3237769, L/Cpl, Pioneer Corps. Killed on the *Lancastria* following evacuation from Dunkirk, 17/7/40.

LAINTON, Leonard, 13069817, Pte, Pioneer Corps. Died in the UK as a result of enemy action, 12/1/41.

LAWE, Norman Edward, 762154, LAC, RAFVR. Died Singapore, 29/11/43.

LEAVER, Dennis Kenny, 748367, Sgt/Pilot, 254 Sqn RAF. KIA 6/12/40 KE, WX. Runnymede Memorial, Surrey, UK Panel 16.

LEE, Walter, LP*.

LEES, Reginald George, 1214347, Sgt Pilot, RAF. Died UK 29/9/43 KE*.

MACHIN, Cyril Henry, Lt, North Staffs. Regt. DoW Burma, 11/6/44.

MANKTELOW, Thomas James, 2049678, Pte, 1st Bn, Royal East Lancs. Regt. KIA France, 27/5/40, EE.

MANNION, Arthur, 4918694, Pte, 2nd Airborne Bn, South Staffs. Regt. KIA Cassino, 9/7/43, EE.

MANSELL, Eric John, 14654727, Pte, 7th Hampshire Regt. KIA Normandy, 6/8/44, EE.

MARSLAND, Kenneth, 127310, FO, 424 Sqn RAFVR. KIA Malta, 29/6/43. Malta Memorial, Malta, Panel 6, Column 2.

MATTHEWS, Alfred, LP*.

MEREDITH, Dennis William, D/MX7228004, PO, HMLC I (L) 252, RN. Died of pneumonia in India, 28/4/45*.

MILLER, Max Ellis Chaplin, Lt-Cmdr, HM Trawler *Lord Stamp*, RN. KIA 14/10/40, KE*, Lowestoft Naval Memorial, Suffolk, UK Panel 1, Column 2.

MONCUR, Gilbert James, 113425, Lt, 1st Bn, Argyll & Sutherland Highlanders. Died Sudan, 17/11/41.

MORLEY, Leslie Edward, 5125510, Gnr, RA. Died UK, 23/2/46.

MOSELEY, John William, 643677, Cpl, Flight Engineer, 110 (Hyderabad) Sqn RAF. KIA over Quetta, India, 21/4/43. Before the war Moseley was a member of the Stafford Battery, RA.

MURRAY, Arthur William, 6473300, Fus., 1st Bn, Royal Fusiliers. KIA Syria, 16/6/41.

Casualties of War

MYATT, Clarence Hulme, Pilot under training, LAC, RAF. Died South Africa, 5/10/42, KE*.

NORLEY, Frank, 2321623, WO II, Royal Signals. Died 6/4/43. Rangoon Memorial, Myanmar, Face 3.

OWEN, Aubrey Sidney, 14273835, Spr, 970 Port Floating Equipment Coy, RE. KIA Normandy, 10/6/44.

OWEN, John Sturdee, Spr, RE. KIA at sea, 1943, EE.

PALMER, Frederick Henry Leighton (Richard on St Albans Plaque), 4920091, Cpl, REME. Died in a motorcycle accident in the UK, 6/9/43, St Alban's Plaque*.

PAPE, Donald Frank Palmer, 1575142, Sgt, 104 Sqn, RAFVR. KIA Alamein, 25/8/43, EE.

PETERS, Henry Joseph, 3201190, Dvr, 922nd Gen. Transport Coy, RASC. KIA Alamein, 24/6/42.

Driver Henry Joseph Peters served with the 922nd Company and was killed during the battle of El Alamein on 24 June 1942.

PLANT, Frank Douglas, P/SMX22, ERM, HM Submarine *Perseus*, RN. KIA Mediterranean, 19/12/41.

POINTON, Frederick Thomas, 14363505, Pte, 5th Bn, Durham Light Infantry. KIA Groesbeek, 23/11/44.

POINTON, George Edward, 44975217, Pte, 4th Bn, Shropshire Light Infantry. KIA Germany, 1/4/45.

POLLARD, David Russell, Lt. KIA Salerno, 11/9/43*.

POOLE, James Malcolm Stuart, DSC and Bar, Lt, HM Submarine *Urge*, RN. KIA Mediterranean, 6/5/42, KE, WX.

POWNER, James Henry, 153204, FO, 115 Sqn, RAFVR. KIA on Dortmund oil plant raid, 15/11/44, KE, EE.

PRICE, Frederick, 525466, Pte, 1st Bn, Worcester Regt. KIA Alamein, 15/10/43.

PRICE, William Henry, 755352, Sgt WOp A/G, 101 Sqn RAFVR. Shot down by Me 109s over target during Brest raid, 24/7/41.

PYE, Henry, 56940, Major, 7th Bn, North Staffs. Regt. KIA during the advance on the West Wall, 8/9/44, WX.

Stafford at War

RACLIFFE, Arthur Cyril, 5122267, Pte, 2nd Bn, Northamptonshire Regt. KIA during invasion of Sicily, 30/7/43. Buried in the Catania War Cemetery, Sicily, Italy, IV, D, 23.

RAY, Elsie, W/89290, L/Cpl, ATS. Died UK, 2/12/45, St Alban's Plaque.

REASON, Dennis William, 748405, Sgt/Pilot, Special Duties Flight, RAFVR. KIA Malta, 23/12/41, KE*.

RIDLEY, Frederick Edward, 41208, PO, 105 Sqn, RAF. KIA Ardennes, 14/5/40, KE, WX*.

ROBINSON, Clifford Reginald, 5050105, Pte, 6th Bn, North Staffs. Regt. KIA Normandy, 6/8/44, EE.

ROBINSON, William, 1903094, Spr, 655 Gen. Construction Coy, RE. KIA in retreat to Dunkirk, 26/5/40.

SADLER, Samuel J., 5121479, Pte, 3rd Bn, Parachute Regt, AAC. KIA Tunisia, 21/3/43.

SALT, George William, 7046341, Royal Irish Fusiliers. Died UK, 30/1/41.

SEDGEWICK, Walter Carloss (C. on EE), 761422, Pte, ROAC. KIA Egypt, 31/8/41, EE.

SHELLEY, Frederick John Francis, P/SSX34049, Able/S, HMS *Fidelity*, RN. KIA, lost in the Atlantic, 1/1/43.

SHERWIN, Robert White, 1043275, Sgt, RAF. KIA 6/9/42 KE*. Runnymede Memorial, Surrey, UK, Panel 93.

SHUKER, Geoffrey Charles, 7655206, S/Sgt, RAOC. Died of illness contracted at HQ, Cairo, 2/11/44, KE.

SILVESTER, Charles Richard, C/JX172055, A/ofS, SS *Ville de Tamatave*, RN. KIA 24/1/43, EE, Chatham Naval Memorial, Kent, UK, 70.3.

SIMMS, Herbert William Charles, 957593, Sgt A/G, 100 Sqn RAFVR. KIA on Hamburg raid, 3/8/43.

SIMPKINS, Leslie, C/KX13352259, Able/S, HM Motor Torpedo Boat 108, RN. Died UK, 6/2/43, St Alban's Plaque.

SIMPSON, Leonard, 1828554, Gnr, 48th Light AA Regt, RA. Died Indonesia, 1/3/42.

SMITH, Gordon John Leslie, 172976, PO, 57 Sqn, RAFVR. KIA on Schweinfurt raid, 27/4/44, EE.

SMITH, John Simmonds, 1232252, F/Sgt, 248 Sqn, RAFVR. KIA 3/9/43 WX.* Runnymede Memorial, Surrey, UK, Panel 139.

SMYTH, Frank Joseph C., 5573478, Pte, 4th Bn, Royal Norfolk Regt. Killed on the Death Railway, 23/8/43, KE.

Casualties of War

SPLANE, Edgar Charles, 154056, FO Nav., RAFVR. Killed in air accident, 26/6/44*.

STARKEY, Charles Frank, 88701, FO, 114 Sqn, RAFVR. KIA 15/6/41, EE. Runnymede Memorial, Surrey, UK, Panel 34.

STOKES, Harold Victor, 2223471, Sgt, 138 Sqn, RAF. KIA, shot down by night-fighter on Potsdam raid, 15/4/45.

STONEMAN, John Stafford, 13368551, WO/Pilot, 103 Sqn, RAFVR. KIA Hamburg raid, 3/8/43, KE, WX.

John Stafford Stoneman attended King Edward VI Grammar School before joining the RAFVR. He flew Lancaster Mark I bombers with 103 Squadron and was killed on the Hamburg raid of 3 August 1943.

STURGESS, Major Victor, P/KX95156, Stoker 1st Class, HM Submarine *Sickle*, RN. KIA 18/6/44, Portsmouth Memorial, Hampshire, UK, Panel 86, Column 2.

SUTTON, Douglas, P/SSX, 11822996, Able/S, HMS *Whitshed*, RN. KIA Dunkirk Operations, 31/7/40.

SWINNERTON, Samuel G., 2618872, Gdsm, 6th Bn, Grenadier Guards. KIA Tunisia, 17/3/43, KE.

TALBOT, Jack, 964697, F/Sgt, 252 Sqn, RAF. KIA 9/5/43, KE, El Alamein Memorial, Egypt, Column 270.

TAYLOR, Alfred William, 50919, Sgt, RAF. Died India, 18/4/42, EE.

THOMAS, Bernard Alphonso, 7960282, Tpr, 43rd Regt Reconnaissance Corps, RAC. KIA Operation Goodwood, 24/6/44.

THOMAS, Sidney Bert, 894418, Gnr RA. Died UK, 7/11/40.

TIPTON, Arthur Owen, 4918702, Pte, 4th Bn, King's Shropshire Light Infantry. DoW as PoW, Germany, 23/10/44.

TYLER, Derek William, 14499439, Pte, 9th Bn, Royal Warwicks. Died UK, 17/2/44.

UNDERHILL, Kenneth James, 1810713, Gnr. Singapore, 12/9/44*.

WAIN, Reginald Sidney, 14654376, Pte, 13th Bn, Parachute Regt. KIA Normandy, 6/6/44.

Reginald Sidney Wain served in the 13th Parachute Regiment and was killed on D-Day.

WAKEFIELD, Joseph, 4968652, Cpl, 9th Bn, King's Shropshire Light Infantry. KIA in the advance on Tunis, 24/4/43.

WALCHESTER, William James, 145292773, Pte, 1st Bn, Herefordshire Regt and King's Shropshire Light Infantry. KIA in the German counter-attack at Anzio, 20/2/44, Anzio War Cemetery, Italy, III, N 3.

WALKER, Arthur K., Sub Lt, HMS *Grebe*, RNVR. KIA 31/3/43, LP*. Lee-on-Solent Memorial, Hampshire, UK, Bay 4, Panel 7.

WALL, Kenneth D., 5050294, Pte, 2nd Bn, Seaforth Highlanders. KIA in the Netherlands, 28/10/44, EE.

Kenneth D. Wall of the 2nd Seaforth Highlanders, a former employee of the English Electric Company, was killed in the Netherlands on 28 October 1944.

WALL, Sidney, 7045928, Fus., 1st Bn, Royal Inniskilling Fusiliers. KIA Rangoon, 7/4/43, St Alban's Plaque.

WALTON, Geoffrey, 1157841, F/Sgt Pilot, RAFVR. Died UK, 15/1/45, KE.

WETTON, Ernest, 4037768, Pte, 4th Bn, King's Shropshire Light Infantry. KIA Normandy, 3/8/44.

WHITE, George Desmond, 748121, Sgt/Pilot, 152 Sqn, RAFVR. KIA Netherlands, 12/8/41, KE.

WHITE, Peter Alfred Cecil, 7360564, S/Sgt, RAMC. Died India, 6/12/45, WX*.

WHITING, Cyril, 5047701, Pte, 2nd Bn, North Staffs. Regt. KIA Anzio, 30/5/44.

WILDING, Laurence Alfred, 5059031, L/Cpl, 6th Bn, Lincoln Regt. KIA Salerno Bridgehead, 23/9/43.

WILKINSON, Charles Frederick, 5053630, Pte, 1st Bn, Gordon Highlanders. KIA Alamein, 25/10/42.

WOOLRICH, Harold, 2736510, L/Cpl, 3rd Bn, Welch Guards. Died UK, 4/6/43.

WRIGHT, Stephen Francis A., P/MX61404, Ld., Sickbay Attendant, HMS *Nile*, RN. Died in Alexandria, where he was on the lab. staff at Alexandria hospital, 9/12/42.

Selected Bibliography

Cull, Brian and Lander, Bruce, with Weiss, Heinrich, *Twelve Days in May* (Grub Street, 1995)

Doherty, Richard, *Normandy 1944* (Spellmount Ltd, 2004)

Gordon, Ed, *HMS Pepperpot* (Robert Hale Ltd, 1985)

Hastings, Max, *Overlord* (Michael Joseph Ltd, 1989)

Hastings, Max, *The Oxford Book of Military Anecdotes* (Guild, 1968)

Jappy, M.J., *Danger UXB* (Channel 4 Books, 2001)

Keegan, John, *Six Armies in Normandy* (Pimlico, 1982)

Middlebrook, Martin, *The Nuremberg Raid 30/31 March 1944* (Fontana, 1975)

Playfair, I.S.O. et al, *The Mediterranean and Middle East. Vol. 4: The Destruction of the Axis Forces in Africa* (HMSO, 1966)

Turner, John, *Periscope Patrol* (Airlife Publishing Ltd, 1997)

Stafford Advertiser (various editions 1937–46)

Stafford Chronicle (various editions 1937–46)

The following unpublished material has also been used

1. Interview notes and correspondence with:
Mr J. Bambury, Mr Bernard Blakeman, Squadron Leader David Blomeley DFC, AFC, Mr D. Challinor, Major Clarke, Mr George Crewe, Mrs Nellie Downing, Squadron Leader Eric Johnson BEM, DFC, AFC, Chief Inspector Gordon Ferneyhough, Commander Leslie Gardiner OBE, Squadron Leader Ernest 'Gil' Gilbert, Mr E. Gosling, Mr Clifford Green, Mrs W.B. Knight, Mrs Haughton, Flight Lieutenant R. Ingar, Lady Morgan, Mr T. Myatt DFM, Wing Commander George Nelson-Edwards DFC, Mr F. Rock, Mr Michael Shelley, Mr Bill Silvester, Mr Leslie Talbot, Pilot Officer Joe Willshaw DFC, Mrs Woodward, Wing Commander Robert Wyness DFC, DFM, Captain Zdzislaw Luszowicz.

2. Logbooks
Squadron Leader D. Blomeley DFC, AFC, RAF
Squadron Leader E. 'Gil' Gilbert, RAF
Squadron Leader E. Johnson BEM, DFC, AFC, RAF
Pilot Officer J. Willshaw DFC, RAF
An unpublished ARP log-book (for Hyde, Lea and Copenhall) currently held by Mrs C. Madders.

Index

Index